NEW YORK STATE

Coach™

America's Best for Student Success®

English Language Arts

GRADE 5

Every effort has been made to locate the copyright holders for the selections in this book. The publisher welcomes information leading to the whereabouts of copyright holders for works in this book that have not been acknowledged. Errors or omissions within the selections are unintentional, and the publisher is pleased to make corrections to future printings.

New York State Coach, English Language Arts, Grade 5
77NY
ISBN 10: 1-58620-923-X
ISBN 13: 1-978-1-58620-923-0

Content Development by Triple SSS Press Media Development
Cover Image: The Statue of Liberty. Illustration by Ralph Voltz.

Triumph Learning® 136 Madison Avenue, New York, NY 10016
A Haights Cross Communications, Inc. company

Printed in the United States of America.

10 9 8

Table of Contents

NOTICE: Photocopying any part of this book is forbidden by law.

3

New York State English Language Arts
Performance Indicators

Performance Indicator	Description	Lesson Correlation
READING		
Standard 1		
R.1.a	Locate and use school and public library resources, with some direction, to acquire information	1, 14
R.1.b	Use the table of contents and indexes to locate information	4
R.1.c	Read to collect and interpret data, facts, and ideas from multiple sources	1, 2, 14, 17
R.1.d	Read the steps in a procedure in order to accomplish a task such as completing a science experiment	5
R.1.e	Skim material to gain an overview of content or locate specific information	1, 4, 6, 10, 14
R.1.f	Use text features, such as headings, captions, and titles, to understand and interpret informational texts	4, 6
R.1.g	Recognize organizational formats to assist in comprehension of informational texts	5, 17
R.1.h	Identify missing information and irrelevant information	13
R.1.i	Distinguish between fact and opinion	12
R.1.j	Identify information that is implied rather than stated	9
R.1.k	Compare and contrast information on one topic from multiple sources	14, 17, 24
R.1.l	Recognize how new information is related to prior knowledge or experience	8
R.1.m	Identify main ideas and supporting details in informational texts to distinguish relevant and irrelevant information	2
R.1.n	Make inferences and draw conclusions, on the basis of information from the text, with assistance	9
R.1.o	Determine the meaning of unfamiliar words by using context clues, dictionaries, glossaries, and other resources (Literacy Competency)	4, 7
Standard 2		
R.2.a	Read, view, and interpret literary texts from a variety of genres	27, 28, 29
R.2.b	Define characteristics of different genres	30
R.2.d	Read aloud from a variety of genres; for example, read the lines of a play or recite a poem; use inflection and intonation appropriate to text read and audience	27, 28, 29
R.2.e	Recognize that the same story can be told in different genres, such as novels, poems, or plays, with assistance	31, 32, 33, 35
R.2.f	Identify literary elements, such as setting, plot, and character, of different genres	31, 32, 33, 35
R.2.g	Recognize how the author uses literary devices, such as simile, metaphor, and personification, to create meaning	3, 27, 36, 37, 38, 39
R.2.i	Recognize how different authors treat similar themes	34, 35
R.2.j	Identify the ways in which characters change and develop throughout a story	32
R.2.k	Determine the meaning of unfamiliar words by using context clues, dictionaries, glossaries, and other resources (Literacy Competency)	4, 7

New York State English Language Arts
Performance Indicators

Performance Indicator	Description	Lesson Correlation
READING		
Standard 3		
R.3.a	Evaluate information, ideas, opinions, and themes in texts by identifying - a central idea and supporting details - details that are primary and those that are less important - statements of fact, opinion, and exaggeration - missing or unclear information	2, 12, 13, 21
R.3.b	Use established criteria to analyze the quality of information in text	21
R.3.c	Identify different perspectives, such as social, cultural, ethnic, and historical, on an issue presented in one or more than one text	21
WRITING		
Standard 1		
W.1.a	Use at least three sources of information in writing a report, with assistance	1, 14, 24, 25
W.1.b	Take notes to record and organize relevant data, facts, and ideas, with assistance, and use notes as part of prewriting activities	10, 13, 15, 16, 17
W.1.c	State a main idea and support it with details and examples	2, 18, 41
W.1.d	Compare and contrast ideas and information from two sources	1, 14, 24, 25
W.1.e	Write labels or captions for graphics, such as charts, graphs, and diagrams, to convey information	6
W.1.f	Adopt an organizational format, such as chronological order, that is appropriate for informational writing	5, 16, 17
W.1.g	Use paragraphing to organize ideas and information, with assistance	16, 18
Standard 2		
W.2.a	Develop original literary texts that - use organizing structures such as stanzas and chapters - create a lead that attracts the reader's interest - provide a title that interests the reader - develop characters and establish a plot - use examples of literary devices, such as rhyme, rhythm, and simile - establish consistent point of view (e.g., first or third person) with assistance	40
W.2.b	Write interpretive essays that - summarize the plot - describe the characters and how they change - describe the setting and recognize its importance to the story - draw a conclusion about the work - interpret the impact of literary devices, such as simile and personification - recognize the impact of rhythm and rhyme in poems	41
W.2.c	Respond to literature, connecting the response to personal experience	8, 22, 41
W.2.d	Use resources, such as personal experiences and themes from other texts and performances, to plan and create literary texts	8, 15, 34, 4

New York State English Language Arts
Performance Indicators

Performance Indicator	Description	Lesson Correlation
WRITING (continued)		
Standard 3		
W.3.a	Use strategies, such as note taking, semantic webbing, or mapping, to plan and organize writing	6, 10, 15, 16, 17
W.3.b	Use supporting evidence from text to evaluate ideas, information, themes, or experiences	2, 18, 19, 23, 24, 41
W.3.c	Analyze the impact of an event or issue from personal and peer group perspectives	8, 21, 23, 41
W.3.d	Analyze literary elements in order to evaluate the quality of ideas and information in text	21, 22, 41
W.3.e	Use information and ideas from other subject areas and personal experiences to form and express opinions	8, 21, 22, 23
W.3.f	Adapt an organizational format, such as compare/contrast, appropriate for critical analysis and evaluation, with assistance	5, 16, 17, 23
W.3.g	Use precise vocabulary in writing analysis and evaluation, with assistance	20
Applicable Core Performance Indicators		
W.CPI.5	Use the writing process (e.g., prewriting, drafting, revising, proofreading, and editing)	15, 16, 19, 20
W.CPI.7	Observe the rules of punctuation, capitalization, and spelling, such as - punctuation of compound sentences, friendly/business letters, simple dialogue, and exact words from sources (quotations); use italics/ underlining for titles - capitalization of proper nouns such as key words in literary and/or book titles, languages, and historical events - spelling of commonly misspelled words, homonyms, and content-area vocabulary	20, 25, 26, 42, 45, 46, 47, 49
W.CPI.8	Use correct grammatical construction in - parts of speech such as nouns; adjectives and adverbs (comparative/superlative); pronouns (indefinite/nominative/objective); conjunctions (coordinating/subordinating); prepositions and prepositional phrases; and interjections simple/compound/complex sentences, using, correct subject-verb agreement, verb tense, punctuation, and pronouns with clear antecedents	20, 42, 43, 44, 48, 49

New York State English Language Arts
Performance Indicators

Performance Indicator	Description	Lesson Correlation
LISTENING		
Standard 1		
L.1.a	Follow instructions that provide information about a task or assignment	5, 11
L.1.b	Identify essential details for note taking	2, 10, 11, 13
L.1.c	Distinguish between fact and opinion	11, 12
L.1.d	Identify information that is implicit rather than stated	9, 11
L.1.e	Connect new information to prior knowledge or experience	8, 11
Standard 2		
L.2.a	Distinguish different genres, such as story, biography, poem, or play, with assistance	11, 27, 28, 29
L.2.b	Identify a character's motivation	11, 32
L.2.c	Recognize the use of literary devices, such as simile, personification, rhythm, and rhyme, in presentation of literary texts	3, 11, 27, 36, 37, 38, 39
L.2.d	Use personal experience and prior knowledge to interpret and respond to literary texts and performances	8, 11
L.2.e	Identify cultural and historical influences in texts and performances, with assistance	3, 11, 28
Standard 3		
L.3.a	Form an opinion on a subject on the basis of information, ideas, and themes expressed in presentations	11, 12, 21, 22
L.3.b	Recognize and use the perspective of others to analyze presentations	11, 21
L.3.c	Use prior knowledge and experiences to analyze the content of presentations	8, 11, 21
L.3.d	Recognize persuasive presentations and identify the techniques used to accomplish that purpose, with assistance	11, 21, 22

Letter to the Student

Dear Student,

Welcome to the revised **New York State Coach, English Language Arts, Grade 5.**
This book will help you improve your English Language Arts skills this year. *Coach* also
gives you practice answering the kinds of questions you will see on tests, including the
state test.

The *Coach* book is divided into chapters and lessons. Before you begin the first chapter,
take the Pretest at the beginning of the book. Then you will know what your strengths and
weaknesses are. You can work on your weak skills all year. By the end of the year, you will
have improved. You can show your improvement to your teacher by doing well on the
Posttest at the end of the *Coach* book. The Pretest and Posttest look like your state test, so
they are good practice. You will be ready to take the state test because you will be used
to the way the state test looks and sounds.

The lessons in this book will help you review and practice your skills. They will get you ready
for the tests you will be taking this year. Some of the practice will be in the style of the state
test. You will be answering multiple-choice and short-response questions. You may see
questions like these on your state test. Practicing with these types of questions will give you
a good idea of what you know and what you need to learn.

Here are some tips that will help you as you go through this book and take tests:

- Listen to your teacher's directions.
- When answering multiple-choice questions, read each choice carefully before
  choosing the BEST one.
- When answering short-response questions, think about what you want to say
  before you begin to write.
- Time yourself so that you have enough time to finish the test and check your work.

We hope you will enjoy using *Coach*. Have a fun and rewarding year!

Letter to the Family

Dear Parents and Families,

The *Coach* series of workbooks is designed to prepare your child to master grade-appropriate skills in English Language Arts and to take the New York State English Language Arts Test, which is the test administered each year in the state of New York. In your state, the grade-appropriate skills are called Performance Indicators. These are the skills the state has chosen as the building blocks of your child's education in English Language Arts, and these are the skills that will be tested on the New York State English Language Arts Test. Your child's success will be measured by how well he or she masters these skills.

You are an important factor in your child's ability to learn and succeed. Get involved! We invite you to be our partner in making learning a priority in your child's life. To help ensure success, we suggest that you review the lessons in this book with your child. While teachers will guide your child through the book in class, your support at home is also vital to your child's comprehension.

Please encourage your child to read and study this book at home, and take the time to go over the sample questions and homework together. The more students practice, the better they do on the actual exam and on all the tests they will take in school. Try talking about what your child has learned in school. Perhaps you can show your children real-life applications of what they have learned. For example, you could discuss why reading skills are important in life and how math skills apply to everyday situations.

We ask you to work with us this year to help your child triumph. Together, we can make a difference!

The *Coach* Parent Involvement Pledge

As an involved parent, I pledge to:

- promote the value of education to my child
- inspire my child to read
- discuss the skills my child needs with his/her teachers and principal
- expect my child to successfully fulfill school and homework assignments
- join in school activities and decisions

I hereby pledge my involvement in my child's educational success!

Parent Signature: _____

Student Signature: _____

PRETEST

English Language Arts

BOOK 1

Book 1

Directions

In this part of the test, you will do some reading. Then you will answer questions about what you have read. For the multiple-choice questions, you will mark your answers on the answer sheet. For question 21, you will write your answer directly in the book.

Read this story. Then answer questions 1 through 5.

Your, Amazing Senses

by Victoria Muñiz

Your body is amazing. Each part does something special. Your heart pumps blood. Your lungs help you breathe, and your brain helps you think and understand. Your body also helps you connect with the outside world. For example, imagine you just bit into a peach. Your body tells you that the peach is juicy, sweet, and fuzzy. How does it tell you these things? Through your senses, of course! You have five senses: seeing, hearing, tasting, touching, and smelling. Each is as important as the other. Let's take a closer look at each one.

Sight is probably the sense most people think of first. The ability to see helps you enjoy things, like a sunset or a painting. It also helps you stay out of danger, like avoiding an oncoming car. Your eyes are the part of your body that allows you to see. Here's how it works. Light enters the eye through the lens and  focuses on something called the retina. The retina contains cells called rods and cones. They tell your brain that it's time to see. They also let your brain know if what you're seeing is black and white or in color.

Hearing is another important sense. Like seeing, hearing helps you enjoy the world around you. For example, you can listen to music, bird song, or your best friend. Hearing also helps you stay out of trouble—you can hear the oncoming car as well as see it. You use your ears to hear. Here's how it works. Sound waves enter your ear and make some parts inside vibrate, or tremble. These vibrations alert your brain to "listen up!"—it's time to hear.

When you're hungry, you probably think that taste is the most important sense. But taste doesn't only tell you that pickles are salty or pizza tastes good cold. This sense also keeps you safe by letting you know that something you shouldn't be eating tastes bad. Think of a baby who wants to put everything in her mouth. Through trial and error, the baby slowly learns what tastes yummy (mashed bananas) and what doesn't (dirty socks). The taste buds on your tongue allow you to taste. Did you know there are four main taste sensations—salty, sweet, bitter, and sour. Which one is your favorite?

You may not think of your sense of touch very often, unless you step on a tack or burn your finger. Like the other senses, touch helps keep you safe by warning you of danger. For example, when you feel the tack enter your foot, you pull your foot away. But touch also helps you enjoy the world around you, too. Your sense of touch makes stroking a kitten or jumping into a cold pool on a hot day fun. Special nerves inside your skin help your brain decide if what you are touching is good (a kitten) or bad (a hot stove).

Last but not least is your sense of smell. Like touch, smell may be less on your mind than the other senses—until you sit next to someone wearing too much perfume on the subway. You know that some things smell good, like apple pie, and other things smell bad, like a skunk. But does your sense of smell also keep you out of danger, like your other senses? The answer is yes. Smell helps warn you when things are not right. For example, you know when you smell smoke, a fire is nearby and you need to get out, fast! Special receptors inside your nose give you your sense of smell.

Now you know a little more about your amazing senses. Here's one last amazing fact. If one or more of your senses is not working, the other senses pitch in to help out. For example, a person who cannot see relies on his sense of touch to read and his sense of hearing to navigate a city street. And a person who cannot hear, can "hear" what you're saying by watching your lips move. Amazing!

Go On

1 Why is one sense **not** more important than another?

A   You don't really need any of them.

B   They all have special parts to play in your body.

C   Most people don't think much about their senses.

D   The brain is the most important organ in your body.

2 Read these sentences from the article.

> **For example, a person who cannot see relies on his sense of touch to read and his sense of hearing to navigate a city street.**

In this sentence, what does "navigate" mean?

F   understand

G   see

H   clean

J   move through

3 How is this article organized?

   A It gives events in the order they happen.

   B It uses a question-and-answer format.

   C It describes how your senses work.

   D It gives step-by-step instructions.

4 The article states that your senses

   F help protect you from danger

   G are less important than other parts of your body

   H develop when you're an adult

   J help you breathe

5 After reading this article, you may conclude that the brain

   A helps your body interpret the senses

   B has no connection to the senses

   C helps you remember your dreams

   D is connected only to the sense of hearing

Go On

Directions
Read this poem. Then answer questions 6 through 10.

The Grass

By Emily Dickinson

The grass so little has to do, —
A sphere of simple green,
With only butterflies to brood,
And bees to entertain,

And stir all day to pretty tunes
The breezes fetch along,
And hold the sunshine in its lap
And bow to everything;

And thread the dews all night, like pearls,
And make itself so fine, —
A duchess were too common
For such a noticing.

> duchess = a noblewoman in
> British society; someone who
> has money and power

6 Why does the poet choose grass as the subject of her poem?

F She wants to show us how much fun it would be to have a lazy, carefree life.

G She wants to explain why grass is important to farmers.

H She wants to show how much she knows about plants.

J She wants to share a story about grass with readers.

7 When the speaker in the poem says, "And stir all day to pretty tunes/The breezes fetch along," she is telling us that

A the grass knows how to sing

B sometimes the wind blows hard

C the grass looks like it's dancing to music when the wind blows

D people should listen more carefully to the wind

8 When the poet writes that the grass "holds the sunshine in its lap," she **most likely** means that

F the grass shines even at night

G the grass shines brightly in the sun

H the sun admires the grass

J the grass needs the sun to grow

9 The speaker compares the grass to a duchess to show that

A the grass is more beautiful

B the duchess likes the grass

C the grass likes expensive jewelry

D the duchess and the grass are exactly alike

10 The poet uses descriptive language to create a sense of

F anxiety

G comedy

H danger

J freedom

Go On

Directions
Read this letter to the editor of a local paper. Then answer questions 11 through 15.

Dear Editor,

It's no secret that cities are noisy places. The large number of people and cars packed into one place raises the noise level. I fully support a law to lower the noise pollution in this city. However, as I'll show in three points, it's unfair of the city to force the Happy Treats ice cream trucks to turn off their cheerful music, when so many others are allowed to make noise.

First, the Happy Treats jingle is pleasant to listen to. Happy Treats has been in business for over 40 years. For many, hearing this familiar jingle as the weather turns warmer means that summer has arrived. Young children hear the song and look forward to summer days. You can't say that about the pounding of jack-hammers, the rumbling of air conditioners, or the squealing of air brakes—all noises we hear every day in this city.

Second, while reducing noise might not cost much to a large corporation, Happy Treats is a small, family-owned business. Donna Riggerio, the owner of the company, said that if her company is forced to turn off its music, it will lose customers. Without the jingle, the Happy Treats truck is just another vehicle on the road. Riggerio also said that providing 250 Happy Treats trucks with music boxes that shut off when the trucks stop will cost more than her company makes in a month. If the city does not allow the Happy Treats jingle, it will drive this longstanding, family-friendly company out of business. Is that what we really want?

Third, and most importantly, not allowing the Happy Treats jingle creates a safety problem. When city drivers hear the familiar jingle, they slow down. They know that the jingle means children will be in the street, so they are extra careful. Do we want to see even one child struck down while crossing the street to buy an ice cream treat? I think not.

Some people say that the Happy Treats jingle is the worst form of noise pollution because the song "pounds inside your head like a bad headache." But we need to focus on bigger companies. Make the trucking companies muffle the brakes on their trucks. Make the construction companies stop working during certain hours of the day. Make the air-conditioning companies find quieter air-cooling systems. Leave the summer to ice cream, memories, and Happy Treats.

Sincerely,

Walter Mendoza

Concerned Citizen

Go On

11 According to Walter Mendoza, the Happy Treats jingle

    A   should be played on the radio

    B   makes people sad

    C   helps keep children safe

    D   is the worst form of noise pollution

12 Which information would fit **best** in paragraph 2?

    F   Older people think fondly of their childhoods when they hear the song.

    G   Customers rely on the music box to know when the truck is nearby.

    H   Safety should always be the first concern when making a big decision.

    J   Happy Treats does not have a large budget to advertise its products.

13 The author probably presented his argument in three points in order to

   A teach readers more about the Happy Treats company

   B present his point of view in a way that's easy for readers to follow

   C show the connection between the jingle and summertime

   D persuade other city residents to keep the noise level down

14 The author would probably agree with which statement?

   F Protecting and preserving tradition is important.

   G Only big businesses deserve rights in the city.

   H Noise isn't a problem in the city.

   J Happy Treats should offer free ice cream to anyone who is bothered by its jingle.

15 When the author says "leave the summer to ice cream, memories, and Happy Treats," he wants the city to

   A ignore the problem of noise pollution in the city

   B allow Happy Treats trucks to operate only in the summer

   C make certain hours during the day into a noise-free time

   D fight companies who really create noise pollution and leave Happy Treats alone

Go On

Directions
Read this story. Then answer questions 16 through 21.

Waiting for Daniel
by Sylvia Potter

"**W**e made it!" Bertie shouted as the ferry pulled away.

Nodding, Amelia smiled down at her little sister, not wanting to make her sad. She knew much still lay ahead of them before they could leave Ellis Island and start their new lives in America. Shading her eyes against the glare, Amelia scanned the crowds for her older brother, Daniel. What if he didn't come for them?

Across the harbor, New York City seemed to shine in the sun. The girls had never seen buildings so tall—certainly not in the small village they'd left behind in County Cork, Ireland. Their parents had always dreamed they'd live in America, the "land of opportunity." Three years before, they'd been able to send Daniel to live with relatives in Brooklyn. Times had grown harder in Ireland. The family had lived on nothing much but potatoes. By the time illness struck, both their parents had been too weak to fight it off.

"The first thing I'm going to do when we get to New York is buy a new dress," Bertie said happily.

"Oh, are ya now? And use what for money?" Amelia laughed at her younger sister, still so naïve, thinking money would no longer be a problem for them. They'd spent everything on their fare across the ocean. Amelia had even taken on extra work as a laundress to earn the final bit.

"Danny will have plenty of money for us," Bertie tossed her strawberry blonde curls. "You'll see."

Amelia swallowed hard. Bertie didn't know that Amelia hadn't heard from Daniel in months. He hadn't answered her last two letters—letters that told him they were coming to America. Amelia had heard that girls needed a male relative to leave Ellis Island, or they'd be sent back to their home country. She shivered at the thought.

They spent the night in a large room with hundreds of other newly arrived immigrants. Clutching her pillow, Amelia lay awake, listening to Bertie's soft snoring. Why hadn't Daniel written back? Was his life in America already too full to include his two sisters? Was he sick or hurt?

It would break Bertie's heart to return to Ireland. She really thought feather beds and velvet gowns awaited her on the other shore. Amelia doubted her sister could survive a trip back. Her cough had grown worse, and she had dark circles under her eyes. Amelia, on the other hand, was "made of stronger stuff," as her mother used to say. Now, she had taken on the role of mothering her sister.

The next morning, officials brought the sisters to the main building. Bertie fidgeted on the wooden bench in the Registry Room. "Why hasn't Danny come yet?" she asked, scanning the faces of the people behind the barrier.

"I'm sure he'll be along soon," Amelia tried to sound cheerful, but she hoped they wouldn't call their names before Daniel had arrived. Amelia accepted a banana from an official, peeled it, and bit into the soft, sweet fruit. It was the first banana of her life. Earlier, she'd watched the other immigrants carefully to see how to eat the fruit. It tasted like America, and she thought it was delicious.

"O'Shaughnessy," a voice suddenly called out their name.

Go On

Bertie clapped her hands while Amelia turned pale. They hurried to follow an official into a separate room where four men sat behind a large desk.

"What do you plan to do in America?" one of the men asked.

Bertie opened her mouth, but Amelia shushed her, "Let me handle this."

"Well, sir, I worked as a maid back home and can do the same work here."

"Do you have a position lined up for yourself?"

"Well, no sir, not yet." Amelia felt her palms grow sweaty.

"That's not good enough. You can't be a burden on society here," one of the men said sternly.

"Isn't anyone here for you girls?" another man asked more kindly.

"Danny, our brother," Bertie blurted out. "He'll be here any minute."

"Well where is he, then?"

Amelia felt her heart sinking. Danny wasn't coming after all. "Bertie," she said softly.

"I'm sorry ladies, but without a male relative to claim you, you'll need to go back home."

"But this is our home now," Bertie cried. "Amelia, tell them!"

An official led them away from the desk and into a long hallway lined with benches. Amelia tried not to look at Bertie or hear her sobbing. She'd led her sister all the way to America only to fail. What would her parents think of her now? Ducking her head to hide her tears, Amelia nearly tripped over the feet of the young man waiting quietly on a bench just outside the door. Looking up to apologize, Amelia stopped short. She would know that smile anywhere.

16 Which of the following is the **best** explanation for why Amelia hides from Bertie the fact that she doesn't know if Daniel is coming to pick them up?

F   She's mad at her sister.

G   She's afraid of disappointing her younger sister.

H   She's worried that Bertie might embarrass her.

J   Her mother asked her not to tell.

17 Amelia thought the banana "tasted like America" because

A   it was a new fruit she'd never tasted before

B   she knew bananas grew on farms in America

C   Daniel had written her a letter all about bananas

D   other immigrants were eating them

18 Now that Amelia and Bertie have found Daniel, what will probably be their next goal?

F   to buy a pretty dress for Bertie

G   to return to Ireland

H   to find work in America

J   to help Daniel find an apartment

19 The setting of the story describes a time period in which

A   few people traveled to America

B   dinosaurs still roamed the earth

C   people traveled by rockets to the moon

D   many people wanted to come and live in America

20 Read this sentence from the story.

Amelia laughed at her younger sister, still so naïve, thinking money would not longer be a problem for them.

In this sentence, the word "naïve" means

F   guilty

G   mean

H   innocent

J   angry

Go On

21 Although she isn't sure if Daniel knows they're coming, Amelia leads her sister to America. Why do you think she does this? Use details from the story to support your answer.

_____

_____

_____

_____

_____

STOP

PRETEST

English Language Arts

BOOK 2

TIPS FOR TAKING THE TEST

Here are some suggestions to help you do your best:

* Be sure to read carefully all the directions in the test book.
* Plan your time.
* Read each question carefully and think about the answer before choosing or writing your response.

Book 2: Part 1

Book 2

Part 1: Listening

Directions

In this part of the test, you are going to listen to an article called "Chores in Colonial America." Then you will answer some questions about the article.

You will listen to the article twice. The first time you hear the article, listen carefully but do not take notes. As you listen to the article the second time, you may want to take notes. Use the space below and on the next page for your notes. You may use these notes to answer the questions that follow. Your notes on these pages will NOT count toward your final score.

For the multiple-choice questions, you will mark your answers on the answer sheet. For questions 26 and 27, you will write your answers directly in the book.

Notes

Go On

Notes

STOP

Book 2: Part 1

Do NOT turn this page until you are told to do so.

22 Which sentence from the article states an **opinion**?

A Hundreds of other tasks needed to be done every week in all seasons.

B By the age of three, children began helping out by performing simple chores.

C Today, children have much better lives than they did in colonial times.

D Until they could walk, all babies also wore very long gowns.

23 The style and wording of the article show that the author is

F trying to make the reader laugh

G asking the reader to change his or her opinion

H giving the reader advice

J explaining something

24 The web below describes chores that colonial children did year-round.

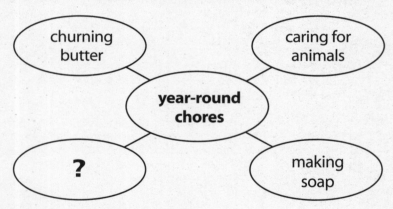

Which phrase **best** completes the web?

A preserving fruit

B weeding gardens

C mending clothes

D clearing land

25 Which word **best** describes what life was like for colonial children?

F fun

G easy

H relaxing

J difficult

26 Describe two ways childhood in colonial America was different than it is today. Use details from the article to support your answer.

_____

_____

_____

_____

_____

Book 2

Part 2: Writing

Sample

There are some mistakes in this paragraph. Let's correct them together.

> Joachim agreed to take a Paper Delivery Route without thinking it through first. If he had, he would have remembered that his bike was broken. His father had actually called it "unfixable" when he sees it after the accident. Joachim wondered how he would be able to deliver fifty papers to fifty different houses within an hour. On foot. If it wasn't fourth of July weekend, he might be able to ask his friends for help.

27 Here is a paragraph that a student wrote. There are some mistakes in the paragraph. Some sentences may have more than one mistake, and other sentences may contain no mistakes at all. There are <u>no</u> mistakes in spelling.

Read the paragraph and find the mistakes. Draw a line through each mistake in the paragraph. Then write the correction above it.

Walt whitman remain one of America's greatest poets. He was born in 1831 in Huntington New York. He spend his early Childhood on Long Island before moving with his' family to Brooklyn. At the age of 11, Whitman leaves school to go to work as an office boy. This was not uncommon at the time. He held many jobs during his life, including teacher, journalist carpenter, and editor.

STOP

Reading and Writing for Information

GETTING THE IDEA

Throughout your life you will read different types of writing for a variety of reasons. Sometimes you will read for pure enjoyment. Other times you will read to learn something new. This unit will focus on nonfiction writing. You will learn strategies for reading and responding to informational texts.

In the following seven chapters, this Unit will help you:

- identify the features of different types of nonfiction texts
- identify the main idea and supporting details of a passage
- understand the different types of word choices used by authors
- understand text format, organization, and graphic organizers
- use prior knowledge and experience as a reading and writing strategy
- make inferences and draw conclusions
- listen effectively and take notes
- distinguish between fact and opinion
- choose the best texts for your purpose and distinguish between essential (important) and nonessential (less important) information
- produce your own writing, including informative and persuasive essays, book and movie reviews, and research reports
- plan your writing, using a number of prewriting techniques

By the end of this Unit, you will be prepared to read informative works and to write your own. Let's get started!

Performance Indicators: R.1.a, R.1.c, R.1.e, W.1.a, W.1.d

CHAPTER

1

Reading for Information

Lesson 1: Reading a Variety of Texts

When you are reading for information, you will likely use an **informational text**. There are many types of informational texts, all of which have the purpose of educating the reader. Examples of informational texts include your classroom textbooks, magazine and newspaper articles, atlases, encyclopedias, dictionaries, CD-ROMs, and other reference materials.

A textbook provides information about one specific subject (such as science, English, or mathematics) and is intended for use in the classroom by a student. Textbooks may be hardcover or paperback and are generally published every few years. Textbooks use features such as headings and illustrations to help guide you and to highlight or summarize certain information. Illustrations are especially helpful if you're a visual learner—that is, if you learn better when you see something as well as read about it.

40

Read the passage below, and then answer the question that follows.

Building the Erie Canal

In 1817, New York Governor DeWitt Clinton gained approval for $7 million in funding to dig a canal from Albany on the Hudson River to Buffalo on Lake Erie. The Erie Canal was begun that same year, and nearly all of the labor for the Canal was performed by men and horses. When it was finished in 1825, the Erie Canal was 363 miles long, 40 feet wide, and 4 feet deep. Within 15 years of the Canal's opening, New York Harbor became the nation's leading port.

What is the main topic of the textbook from which this passage would most probably be taken?

_____

_____

_____

HINT! What kind of passage is it? Literature? History? Science?

Some other reference materials you might use are described below and on the following pages.

An **atlas** is a book of maps, and you could use one to locate a particular place. A U.S. atlas has maps of just the United States; a world atlas would have maps of every country in the world. A road atlas has maps of the roads in a specified place. You might look in an atlas to find out what countries border Brazil or what routes you might take from Albany to Niagara Falls.

A **dictionary** is a book-length alphabetical list of words and their pronunciation, definition, and origins. You've probably used a dictionary to look up the definition of a word. You would use a dictionary to find the meaning of the word ingest, or to find out which language the word ingénue comes from.

You may have used an encyclopedia to do research. **Encyclopedias** provide alphabetical listings of topics with a short article on each. An encyclopedia could be one long book, or a series of books called volumes. There are general encyclopedias and more specific ones, such as encyclopedias of science, of technology, and even of music. You might turn to a general encyclopedia for information about a country, its history, population, industry, and so on.

A **thesaurus** is a book-length alphabetical list of words that gives their synonyms (words with similar meanings) and antonyms (words with opposite meanings). If you wanted to find a word with the same meaning as *angry*, you would use a thesaurus, and look for synonyms of *angry*. Or, if you wanted to know what word means the opposite of *cherish*, you could find this in a thesaurus.

Many of the nonfiction texts we've learned about are published every few years. For example, a new edition of a dictionary might come out every five years. A new set of encyclopedias appears even less often. Some informational texts, called periodicals, are published more frequently. A **periodical** is a publication that is published at regular time intervals, such as daily, weekly, or every two months. Some examples of periodicals you should be familiar with are newspapers and magazines. A newspaper is a daily or weekly publication that includes reports on local, national, and international events as well as opinion articles and feature stories. You might find an article about local politics, an editorial arguing that a library should not be closed, help-wanted listings, and the latest sports news, all in the same newspaper.

Some reference materials are available as CD-ROMs. This abbreviation stands for Compact Disc-Read Only Memory. A **CD-ROM** is a disc of reference information used on your computer; dictionaries and encyclopedias are often available in a CD-ROM format. CD-ROMs can hold 650MB of data, which is equal to about 250,000 pages of text. The information on a CD-ROM cannot be changed or erased.

You are probably familiar with the **Internet**, which can be a very useful resource. The Internet is an electronic collection of sources that you can reach through a computer. You can find all of the other sources we've been discussing here on the Internet—there are atlases, newspapers, encyclopedias, and much more. Many of these are free, although some charge readers a fee to view articles or texts. You have to be careful when using the Internet, and check the source of the information you find. Not everything on the Internet is reliable or accurate. Because anyone can post information there, some things may be incorrect. Look for trustworthy sources, such as government sites (these websites will end in .gov), education sites (colleges and universities; these websites will end in .edu), and other reputable organizations, such as well-known newspapers (the *New York Times* or *Washington Post*, for example).

Generally, you can use a search engine such as Google or Yahoo! to find things on the Internet. Just type in the key words about your topic and click on *Go* or *Search*. For example, to find out information on Brazilian frogs, you would type in "Brazilian Frogs." Online references, such as encyclopedias, usually have their own search tools built in. Again, type in your key word and click on the enter key. If you do a search on the Internet for Brazilian frogs, for example, you will come up with tens of thousands of possible websites with information on this topic. It's easy to get lost among those thousands of entries. You can narrow your search by choosing your search words more carefully. If you know that your report will be on frogs of the Brazilian rainforest, add "rainforest" to your search words.

Read the information below, and then answer the question that follows.

www.historysearch.com

www.spacenews.gov

www.fordham.edu

Which of these websites would probably be the <u>least</u> reliable source of information?

_____

_____

_____

HINT! Are any of the sites governmental or educational?

Example 1

1 **In which of the following would you look to find out how to get to Binghamton from Syracuse?**

    A   encyclopedia

    B   dictionary

    C   thesaurus

    D   atlas

 Which informational text provides roadway information?

Example 2

2   **Martine is writing a paper on French mathematician René Descartes. Which of the following would be the BEST source for her research?**

F   an encyclopedia article on France

G   a newspaper article on middle school math test scores

H   a biography of Descartes on the Yale University Web site

J   an Internet article from www.mathworks.com

Which informational text seems most reliable and most clearly connected to Martine's topic?

Example 3

3   **Which of the following would you find in a thesaurus?**

A   the definition of a word

B   the origins of a word

C   translations of words into another language

D   lists of words that have the opposite meaning

A thesaurus is a dictionary of synonyms and antonyms.

Example 4

The Catskill Mountains offer some of the finest outdoor recreation in the United States. Catskill Park is 700,000 acres full of opportunities for campers, hikers, fly fishers, golfers, and skiers. If you're traveling in the fall, go in September or October, and prepare to be delighted by the beautiful colors of the fall foliage in the Catskills. The area also abounds with historical sites, so if the weather won't allow that hike you had planned, check out the historic Dutch homes nearby, and then visit a few of the local antique stores. Have the kids along? Enjoy the great outdoors, of course, but also consider treating them to a visit to one of the area fun parks for go-carts, paddleboats, miniature golf, and water slides. You'll find something for each member of the family in the Catskills, where the fun is year-round.

4 **This passage is most likely from which source?**

F college journal

G atlas

H travel magazine

J encyclopedia

Think about what kind of information the passage provides—which type of publication might provide such information for its readers?

Example 5

galaxy *noun* a very large group of stars and planets.
[Greek, *galaxias*]

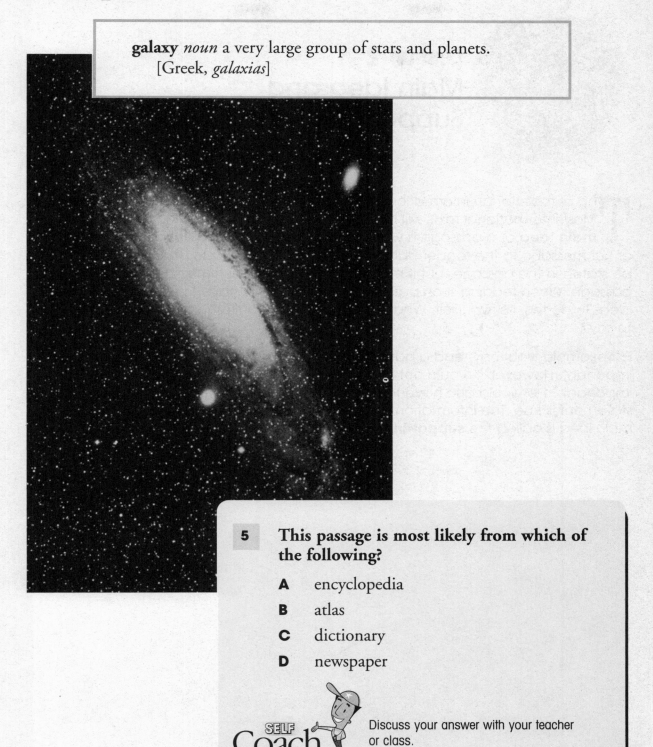

5 **This passage is most likely from which of the following?**

A encyclopedia

B atlas

C dictionary

D newspaper

SELF Coach™ Discuss your answer with your teacher or class.

Performance Indicators: R.1.c, R.1.m, R.3.a, W.1.c, W.3.b, L.1.b

Lesson 2
Main Idea and
Supporting Details

The purpose of an informational text is to provide the reader with information. Most informational texts will have a main idea and supporting details. The **main idea** of a passage is what it is mostly about. The author's main idea is his or her message to the reader about the topic of the passage. The main idea may be stated in the passage, but it might also be *implied*, or hinted at throughout the passage. When reading such passages, the reader will have to figure out the main idea. To do this, ask yourself: What is the passage about? What is the author trying to say?

For example, you may read a passage with the main idea that recycling is important. However, it would not be enough for the author to say, "Recycling is important." He would also have to provide the reader with the reasons *why* this statement is true. The information the author includes to support, or back up, the main idea is called the **supporting details** of the passage.

Read the passage below, and then answer the question that follows.

According to the Environmental Protection Agency (EPA), the average U.S. citizen produced more than 1600 pounds of waste in the year 2000. This adds up to an astonishing annual total of 220 tons of waste. Waste includes everything thrown away, from paper, plastics, and glass to food scraps, yard trimmings, and metals. How much do you throw away, and where does it all go? Thankfully, about 46 tons of waste from 2000 were recycled. What about the other 154 tons? It mostly went into landfills. It's important that Americans recycle more. Recycling saves money, energy, and the environment. Let's reuse products when possible, reduce the waste, and recycle everything we can.

What is the main idea of this passage? Can you name some supporting details?

_____

_____

_____

_____

 What is the passage mostly about? Does the author include information to support the main idea?

When you write, always be aware of what you want the main idea of your writing to be. Think about your topic: What will your passage be about? What main point are you going to make? Plan out how you will organize your ideas, and list the supporting details you will include to present your topic or argument. Diagrams can help you organize your ideas. Look at the diagram of a main idea and supporting details on the next page.

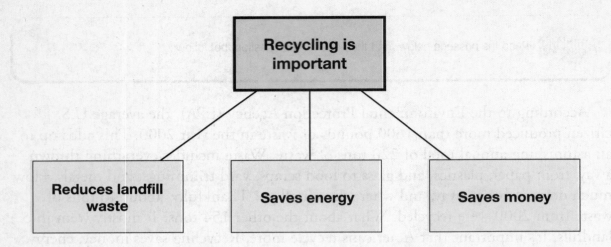

The diagram above is also known as a graphic organizer. You can see at a glance what the main idea is, as well as the supporting details for that main idea. You will learn more about graphic organizers in Lesson 6. Try this example.

Example 1

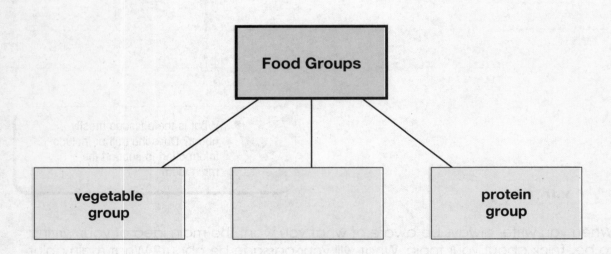

1a **This organizer shows that the main idea of this passage is**

  A vegetable group

  B food groups

  C protein group

  D types of food

Remember that the main topic appears in the top or main box in a graphic organizer.

1b **In the chart, which of the following BEST fits in the empty box?**

  F milk, yogurt, and cheese group

  G protein group

  H broccoli group

  J food groups

The box should not include the same information found in other boxes.

Example 2

ost people have heard of wolves, although few have seen a live wolf in the wilderness. Sadly, wolves have gained a bad reputation that is not totally fair. Although wolves rarely attack humans, many of us expect to be automatically attacked if we should run into a wolf. Part of our fear comes from the image of the wolf in books and movies. Think, for example, of "Little Red Riding Hood." From an early age, people learn to see wolves as sly, dangerous creatures on the hunt for humans.

2a **What is this passage mainly about?**

A People are afraid of wolves.

B Wolves have gained an unfair reputation.

C Most people have read books about wolves.

D "Little Red Riding Hood" didn't really happen.

What is the most important point that the writer is trying to make?

2b **Which of the following is NOT a supporting detail in the passage?**

F People expect wolves to attack them.

G Books help create a fear of wolves.

H Wolves rarely attack humans.

J Wolves are not as dangerous as other wild animals.

Discuss your answer with your teacher or class.

Lesson 3
Understanding Diction

You have a certain way of speaking—there may even be words you use quite often. You probably sound like your family, your friends, and other people around you from whom you learned to talk. The way you speak is called **diction**. Your diction may change when you are speaking with different people. In writing, diction consists of the words the author uses to provide information, tell a story, write a poem, or bring characters to life.

Just as you speak differently with your friends than you might with your grandparents, writers choose their words based on the audience for which their work is intended. You would not use your favorite slang phrases when speaking to your teacher, and your parents would not likely use the formal speech they might use at work when speaking to you at the dinner table. We all adjust our diction—we make different word choices—to suit our audience. If the writer misjudges the audience, the diction in a piece of writing might not appeal to that audience. It might actually make the writing confusing. Using the appropriate diction when you write can help you make a connection with the reader.

Read the passage below, and then answer the question that follows.

Liam looked at his test paper and scowled at his friend, Andrew. "I dunno why I bother to study. I just ain't gonna get this stuff."

How might Liam change his diction if he were talking to his teacher instead of his friend?

_____

_____

_____

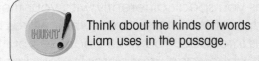

Think about the kinds of words Liam uses in the passage.

There are a few different types of diction. **Informal diction** is the language used in everyday speech. It uses simple, common words, contractions, and slang. **Formal diction** uses more difficult words and often has a more serious, official tone. In between these two is **middle diction**, which uses words correctly, but is not as serious or complex as formal diction.

An author might use formal diction to appeal to a well-educated audience, or to make her story's characters appear smart, sophisticated, or highly educated. In contrast, an author might choose very relaxed, conversational informal diction—simple words, even slang—to suggest that his characters are average, down-to-earth people or to appeal to a less formal audience. Most newspapers use middle diction. They use standard English and correct grammar, but they want to appeal to a general audience. Therefore, they tend to avoid diction that would be too complicated or difficult for their readers.

Example 1

1. Dogs are really great. They make cool pets and are really reliable. They are very loyal and smart, too. If you're lucky enough to have a dog, you know what I mean.

2. All dogs belong to the *canid* family (family *Canidæ*). *Canids* are the earliest known carnivores: dogs first appeared in the fossil record about 40 million years ago. The domestic dog's closest relative is the gray wolf (*Canis lupus*).

1a **Which of the following best describes the diction of passage 1?**

   A formal

   B middle

   C informal

   D basic

What kind of word choices does the author of this passage make?

1b **What differences do you see in the diction of the two passages? Give specific examples.**

_____

_____

_____

_____

Compare the types of words used in these two passages. How do they differ?

Example 2

If you develop an interest in baking, you might want to research books on cooking at your local library. A librarian and the library database are certain to be of assistance. Resolve beforehand on the type of cooking you might wish to do. Perhaps it is your greatest desire to bake the American standard apple pie.

Begin your baking experience by preparing your kitchen. Ascertain in advance the ingredients and equipment needed for the recipe, and make purchase of these prior to your baking engagement. Thus prepared, and by following your chosen recipe stringently, you will undoubtedly create a most appetizing dessert.

2 **What is the diction of this passage? Is it appropriate to the subject matter? Explain why or why not, using examples from the passage.**

_____

_____

_____

Discuss your answer with your teacher or class.

Coached Reading

This article is about a school soccer team and its coach. As you read the article, use the statements and questions in the margin to help your understanding.

 Your teacher may read this selection to you.

Local sports fans are rejoicing today. On Monday evening, the St. Albans Tigers girls' soccer team played its way through the semifinal match against the Lockwood Lions, winning the match 3-1 and advancing to the state finals.

It wasn't a certain win, and the Tigers worked hard, trailing the Lions in the first half of the game. Then, in an amazing burst of energy, the Tigers rallied and scored two goals in three minutes, and then scored a third with only seconds left in the game. Two of the team's three goals were scored by Dani Redmond, assisted by Michelle Rothberg. The third was carried by Sophia Littman.

It's the first time in five years that St. Albans has had a team in the state finals in any sport. Team captain Michelle Rothberg says her team's success is due to the efforts of her coach, Linda Ramirez.

> What is this passage mainly about so far?

> What is the most likely source for this passage? A textbook? A dictionary?

"We couldn't have made it so far without our great coach, Miss Linda," said an overjoyed Rothberg after Monday's win. "She guided us to this point all year, and worked us so hard, but it was worth it, really, and we all just want to say thanks to her for her support and her belief in us as a team."

Coach Ramirez is the 10th-grade biology teacher at St. Albans, and has coached the girls' varsity soccer team for the past two years. She took the position upon the retirement of the team's beloved longtime coach, Reggie Martin. Martin is excited about the Tigers' prospects for a state championship:

How would you describe the diction of this section of the passage?

"I talked with Coach Ramirez just last week, and I've been down to the field to watch the team practice now and then. I just love the game. Let me tell you, these are some of the hardest working girls I've ever seen, and I've coached a lot of teams over the years. Used to be the girls had other things on their minds, distractions, you know, but these girls of Linda's, they've got a one-track mind, and it's all soccer!"

How is the diction of this paragraph different from the diction of the paragraph before it?

Martin guided the Lady Tigers for 14 of his 22 years at St. Albans, and led them to the state finals three times in those years, though the team never secured the state title. Coach Ramirez hopes to help the Tigers break through that glass ceiling, and carry them to the top this year.

"This is the most committed and enduring group of young women you will ever encounter," said Coach Ramirez of her team. "Sure, they have talent, but they know that it takes more than natural ability to succeed—you need discipline. You have to work hard and consistently. You have to pick yourself up after a defeat, and get right out there working hard, sweating through your tears. Let me tell you, these girls are ready to win."

If Monday night's game is any indication, Coach Ramirez's Tigers certainly are ready to win. St. Albans is planning a pep rally for the team on Friday at 1:30 p.m. in the gymnasium, and it's open to the public. Come down and cheer your local team, and help them bring the state title back to St. Albans. You'll find the results here in Sunday's sports section.

> What is the main idea of this paragraph?

> What are some supporting details from the passage?

Re-read the article, and ask yourself the questions in the margin again. Then answer questions 1 through 4.

1 **This passage is most likely from a**

  A thesaurus

  B academic journal

  C newspaper

  D textbook

2 **The passage is mainly about**

  F Coach Martin's history at St. Albans

  G Michelle Rothberg's job as team captain

  H local sports teams

  J the St. Albans girls' soccer team

3 **Which of the following is a supporting detail from the passage?**

  A The Tigers are disciplined and focused.

  B Coach Ramirez teaches biology.

  C The Lions beat the Tigers.

  D Team members played poorly when Reggie Martin was the coach.

4 **Briefly describe the diction of the passage. Use examples from the passage.**

_____

_____

_____

_____

_____

NOTICE: Photocopying any part of this book is forbidden by law.

61

Test Practice

> **Read this article about an event in history. Then answer questions 1 through 3.**

The Buffalo Expo

The city of Buffalo was the site of the Pan-American Exposition of 1901. The Expo began in May of 1901 and ran through November of that year, but it had taken three years of preparation to get the Exposition ready. Beginning in 1899, many buildings were built on 342 acres along Buffalo's Grand Canal. They featured exhibits on everything from African-American advancements to gardening to new technology such as electricity. There were African, Eskimo, and Indian villages, and an Electric Tower that was colorfully lit with 20,000 lights.

Theodore Roosevelt, who would become President of the United States later that year, opened the Expo in spring of 1901. The Expo had many exhibits and events. There were also rides at the Expo—the Aerio-Cycle and the Trip to the Moon were both quite popular. Other exhibits for amusement included an upside-down house (just what it sounds like), a Court of Fountains, and Dreamland, a mirror maze. There were also exhibits on Japan and the Orient. A street from the German city of Nuremburg was reproduced, as was the city of Venice, Italy, through which Expo visitors could take a ride on a boat called a gondola.

The Expo was a great success. The population of Buffalo in 1901 was just over 350,000, yet nearly 8 million visitors came to the Buffalo Exposition.

1 The diction of this article is **best** described as

   A formal

   B middle

   C informal

   D secondary

2 The article is **mainly** about

   F how Theodore Roosevelt became president

   G the role of African-Americans at the Pan-American Exposition

   H the 1901 Pan-American Exposition in Buffalo

   J what a great town Buffalo is

3 This article is **most likely** from which of the following?

   A textbook

   B atlas

   C dictionary

   D travel magazine

Read this article. Then answer questions 4 through 6.

Calgary is a really interesting place to visit, and it has a cool history, too. The town was started in 1875, as a fort. Of course, the Blackfoot Indians lived there first, you know. It's in Alberta, on the eastern edge of the Rockies, where these two rivers—the Bow and Elbow—meet up. In 1883, the Canadian Pacific Railway came to town and really shook things up. Loads of settlers started moving in, and before long, Calgary was the hot spot for transport. The government leased lots of land for cattle grazing, and Calgary became cattle center of Canada, too. From 1896 to 1914, the government gave out these totally free homesteads, and tons of people came out for them and started more ranches.

Somebody found oil in 1914, and then people struck oil again in 1947. Major changes happened when big oil reserves were found in the 1960s. The city grew a lot more, but things were kind of up and down just like the oil prices. These days, more than 900,000 people live in Calgary, and it's like the third most populated city in Canada. The Calgary Stampede is a totally fun event there every July—it's a rodeo and festival that was started in 1912. Everyone goes Western for Stampede week, and it links the town to its cattle ranching roots. The cattle town has a modern look these days and modern industries, too.

4 This article is **most likely** from

F a college journal

G an atlas

H a magazine

J a dictionary

5 What is this article **mainly** about? Name at least two supporting details from the passage.

_____

_____

_____

_____

_____

_____

_____

_____

NOTICE: Photocopying any part of this book is forbidden by law.

65

6 Is the diction of the article appropriate? Explain why or why not, using examples from the article.

_____

_____

_____

_____

_____

_____

_____

_____

_____

Performance Indicators: R.1.b, R.1.e, R.1.f, R.1.o, R.2.k

Format and Text Structure

Lesson 4: Understanding Format

The format of a text is how the text is arranged and organized. Writers organize information to make it easier to read and understand. There are a number of ways this is done. The first is by title. The title of a book or article tells the reader what the text is about. When you do research, you may search in a library database for books on a particular topic. Books with titles relating to your topic are more likely to be books you could use in your research. Of course, some authors choose titles that are eye-catching but do not refer directly to the subject of their book or article. That is why you must read beyond the title to find out what a text is really about.

The next level of organization in a book is chapters. Chapters are sections of the book containing information on the same topic. Each chapter of a book will have its own title, which will tell you what that chapter is about.

The titles of the chapters in a book are found in the table of contents, which is another element of text format. The **table of contents** is a list in the front of a book that provides the chapter numbers and titles, as well as the page number each chapter begins on. This list is organized in the order in which the chapters appear.

NOTICE: Photocopying any part of this book is forbidden by law.

67

Read the table of contents below, then answer the question that follows.

Which chapter would you look in to find out when the first New York fire department was set up? What page does it begin on?

_____

_____

_____

 The chapter title tells you the kind of information you will find in the chapter.

Some tables of contents are more detailed than others. Take a look at the table of contents in this book, for example. It includes both the units in the book and the chapter titles within each unit. Then each chapter is divided into smaller parts, the lessons.

Authors also use headings to organize their writing. **Headings** break up sections of text within a larger text. For example, lesson and chapter titles are headings. There can also be headings within lessons. Writers make headings stand out by putting them above the other words on a page, sometimes in bigger letters, or in bold, or underlined. You may have expected this lesson to be about format because of the heading at the beginning of this lesson. A heading can be used to introduce new topics and to break up sections of text that contain a lot of information.

Read the passage below, and then answer the question that follows.

Poison dart frogs are native to the rainforest of Brazil. They were given this name because some native South Americans used their poison to make darts for hunting. The chemicals in the skin of some poison darts frogs are deadly. The chemicals will not go through a person's skin, but can enter the body through a cut in the skin. Many of the poisons in the dart frog's body come from an ant that is part of their regular diet.

What would be a good heading for this section of text?

_____

_____

_____

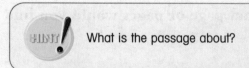 What is the passage about?

Many informational texts will have a glossary. A **glossary** is an alphabetical list of key words and terms used in the book and their definitions. You will find a glossary at the back of this book. Words that appear in the glossary are in bold type, as is the word "glossary" in this paragraph.

Glossaries can be especially helpful when you're reading a text with a lot of specialized terms, like a science textbook. For example, maybe you come across the word "permeate" in a science book, but you're not sure what it means. Check the book's glossary to see if the word is defined there.

Indexes also appear at the back of a book. These are alphabetical lists of subjects mentioned in the book, followed by the page numbers on which the subject is mentioned. If you were doing a report on making kites, but the book in your hands was about kites in general, you wouldn't have to read the entire book to find a few paragraphs on your topic. You could simply look up "making kites" or "kite-making" in the index to find that information in the book. Indexes work like tables of contents to help the reader find information in a book, but indexes are a lot more specific than tables of contents. They break down topics into smaller details.

 Read the passage below, and then answer the question that follows.

Chinese kites, 38, 56–58

history of kites, 35–38, 49

kite festivals, 77, 86

kite-making, 55–59

On what page or pages would you find information on how to make a kite?

_____

_____

_____

 Does this index include an entry on making kites?

Example 1

1a **In which chapter would you find information about kittens?**

A   Chapter 1

B   Chapter 2

C   Chapter 3

D   Chapter 4

Look next to each chapter number in the table of contents to see the chapter's title.

1b **Which page would you look on to find out about snakes?**

F   page 11

G   page 45

H   page 59

J   page 73

Find the chapter title related to snakes in the table of contents, and then look next to it for the page number of the chapter.

Example 2

The Art of Beekeeping

Introduction

Honeybees are essential to the world's food chain. They help create much of the world's food through their main job: pollination. Apiculture, or beekeeping, is the maintenance of bees as a hobby or for commercial purposes. Beekeepers maintain beehives and harvest honey and beeswax from the hives. Bees are commonly kept in a beehive. Commercial hives are made of wood and house from 15,000 to 50,000 bees.

Types of Bees in a Hive

A beehive has one queen whose job it is to lay eggs. She produces male and female eggs. Females become workers, and males become drones. Workers care for eggs, gather nectar, build the honeycomb, and produce the honey in the hive. The purpose of drones is to reproduce with the queen.

Harvesting Hives

Inside the beehive are honeycombs, which are made of beeswax by the worker bees. Beekeepers use smoke to chase the bees from the hive, at which point the honey and the honeycomb are harvested from the hive.

2 **Read the following sentence.**

The queen can lay more than 1,500 eggs each day and has a lifespan of two to eight years.

Under which heading from the passage would this sentence best fit?

F Introduction

G Types of Bees in a Hive

H Harvesting Hives

J Queen Bees

Which section from the passage contains information on the queen bee?

Example 3

You have probably played a number of different board games in your life. Did you know that some board games have been popular for hundreds of years? Back in the Middle Ages, both aristocrats (kings, queens, and other people of the royal class) and commoners enjoyed playing a variety of board games. They played a game called tables, an early version of backgammon, and merrils, a game like tic-tac-toe, only more complicated. Checkers was another common game. However, the most popular board game of all was chess.

3 **A good heading for this passage would be**

   A   How to Play Chess

   B   A History of Backgammon

   C   Popular Board Games of the Middle Ages

   D   Why Board Games Are Fun

SELF
Coach™

Discuss your answer with your teacher or class.

Lesson 5
Understanding Sequence

One of the most common ways writers organize their writing is **chronological order**, or **sequence**. This means that they write about events in the order in which they happened. Directions and instructions are usually written in chronological order. This writing style helps the reader understand what is going on, and why.

When a text is not in the correct order or sequence, it can be very confusing for the reader. This is true of fiction and nonfiction. Read the following passage:

> Once the clothes are in the washer, close the lid, and wait for the washer to reach the rinse cycle, when you will add fabric softener. This will take up to 10 minutes. You should check the washer settings, and adjust them for the load you are washing. This is to make sure that the dyes in darker clothing do not bleed onto lighter clothing. Use hot water for whites, warm for colors, and cold for dark colors. As the washer fills with water, add the laundry detergent, and then add the clothes. You first have to sort the clothes by color, usually into whites, darks, and colors.

You can probably tell that this passage provides instructions for doing laundry, but the information is not presented in the right order. If you tried to follow these instructions as written, you would have a difficult time with your laundry! See how much easier it is to follow in the right order:

> You first have to sort the clothes by color, usually into whites, darks, and colors. You should check the washer settings, and adjust them for the load you are washing. This is to make sure that the dyes in darker clothing do not bleed onto lighter clothing. Use hot water for whites, warm for colors, and cold for dark colors. As the washer fills with water, add the laundry detergent, and then add the clothes. Once the clothes are in the washer, close the lid, and wait for the washer to reach the rinse cycle, when you will add fabric softener. This will take up to 10 minutes.

The chronological method is used in many types of writing. If you were writing the story of your life, where would you begin? Where would your story end? Newspapers, history books, recipes, biographies, and instructional manuals typically use chronological order for organization. Fiction is often organized this way, too.

Words Used in Chronological Writing	
first	later
next	finally
then	afterwards

Example 1

Kavi and Jamar were on a camping trip with Jamar's family. Jamar was telling Kavi how to set up the tent. "First you have to unroll the tent, and sort all the pieces. We have to spread the tent out, and then we put the poles together. Next, we put the poles into the tent, one at a time. Then we each take an end of a pole, and insert the end into that hole at the base of the tent. Once we've done that with each pole, the tent will be up, and we'll just have to stake it."

Kavi looked at Jamar and smiled. "Is that all?" Then he emptied the tent bag out on the ground.

1 **According to the passage, which of the following must Jamar and Kavi do first in order to set up the tent?**

A Put the tent poles in the tent

B Unroll the tent

C Stake the tent

D Spread the tent out

What does Jamar tell Kavi they must do first?

Example 2

1. "Hiya, mister! What can I do for ya?"

2. He heard nothing at first, and then the faint sound of a door opening far away. This was followed by deep, heavy footsteps. He wondered to himself if he should just run off while he had the chance. The heavy footsteps grew closer, and louder, and then the door slowly creaked open.

3. Standing before him, Arthur saw a young boy. He was walking on a pair of homemade stilts, the bases of which were stuck in two big, heavy orthopedic shoes. He couldn't help chuckling to himself as he realized that his first impression had been terribly, terribly wrong.

4. Arthur walked up to the house, looking it over for a moment before ringing the bell. It was a huge structure, likely a grand mansion long ago, but it had obviously fallen into disrepair over the years. Sighing to himself, he stepped forward to ring the bell, and then he waited.

---

2 **Which of the following is the BEST order of these paragraphs, using the chronological method?**

F 1, 3, 4, 2

G 1, 2, 3, 4

H 4, 2, 1, 3

J 4, 3, 2, 1

Discuss your answer with your teacher or class.

Lesson 6
Graphic Organizers

Sometimes, especially in nonfiction writing, you might find it helpful to include a graphic organizer. A **graphic organizer** is a diagram that helps you visualize, or see, ideas that might be difficult to explain in words. Types of graphic organizers include:

- drawings
- photographs
- charts
- tables
- maps
- diagrams
- graphs

Graphic organizers often have **captions** that describe what is shown. A captions is a phrase or short sentence that explains how the graphic is related to the text. When you see a graphic organizer on a page, you can glance at the captions to get a better idea of what the text is about.

Writers use graphic organizers to make their ideas clearer for the reader. Graphic organizers can also help to break up long sections of text. In this lesson, you will learn about some common types of graphic organizers.

Cycle Diagram

A cycle diagram can be used to show a circular process, such as the changing of the seasons.

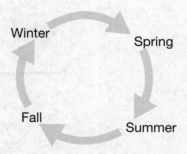

Pyramid Diagram

A pyramid diagram can be used to show a building relationship or how resources should be used, such as with the food pyramid.

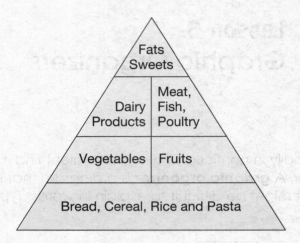

 THINKING IT THROUGH Use the pyramid diagram above to answer the following question.

According to the diagram, which food group should make up the largest part of an individual's diet?

_____

_____

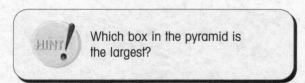

HINT! Which box in the pyramid is the largest?

Radial Diagram

A radial diagram can be used to show how different things relate to one central idea, item, or person.

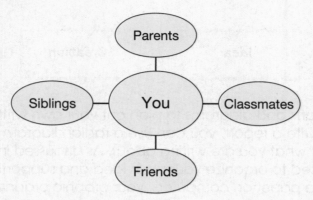

Organizational Chart

An organizational chart can be used to show where things and/or people are situated within an organization.

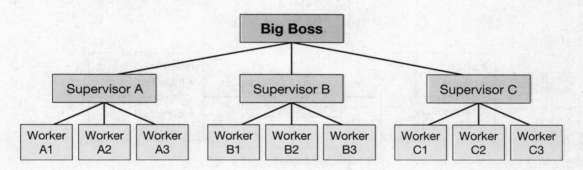

 THINKING IT THROUGH   Use the organizational chart above to answer the following question.

Who directly supervises Worker B3?

_____

_____

_____

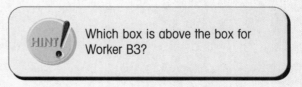

HINT!   Which box is above the box for Worker B3?

Flowchart

A flowchart is used to show how one step in a process leads to another. A flowchart could be used to plan out the order in which you present new information.

You can also use charts and diagrams to plan out your own writing. For example, when preparing to write a report, you can use a radial diagram to help you see the different elements of what you are writing about. As discussed in Lesson 2, graphic organizers can be used to organize your main idea and supporting details. If you were going to write a paper on computers, your graphic organizer might look something like this:

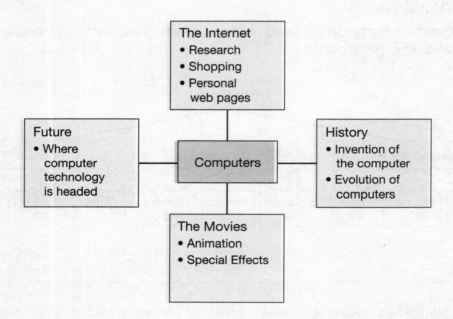

You can also use a graphic organizer to organize the process by which you will do something, a series of instructions, or a sequence of events.

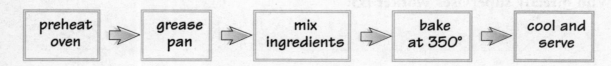

Use the graphic organizer on page 80 to answer the following question.

What should you do after preheating the oven, according to the diagram?

_____

_____

_____

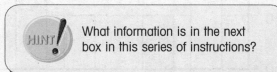 HINT! What information is in the next box in this series of instructions?

Tables

A table is a visual representation of information broken down into columns with headings. Tables list information, making it easier for you to understand it.

Rocks	Material	Location
igneous	magma	deep in the earth
sedimentary	eroded earth materials	bottoms of bodies of water
metamorphic	igneous or sedimentary rocks	Earth's crust

Graphs

A graph is a type of diagram used to show relationships between two or more different amounts. A common type of graph is the bar graph. The one below shows concert ticket sales.

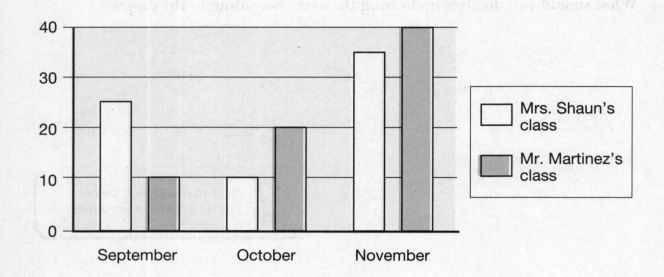

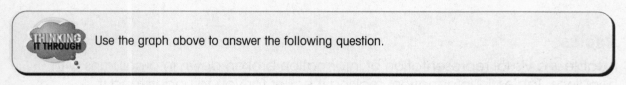
Use the graph above to answer the following question.

Which group sold the most concert tickets in September?

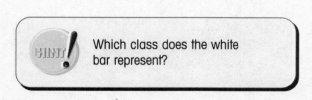
Which class does the white bar represent?

Illustrations and Maps

Other types of graphics are illustrations and maps. Illustrations and maps are drawings that make information in a text clearer. For example, if you were reading about cities in New York, a map of the state, with the cities labeled, would help you to understand what was being discussed.

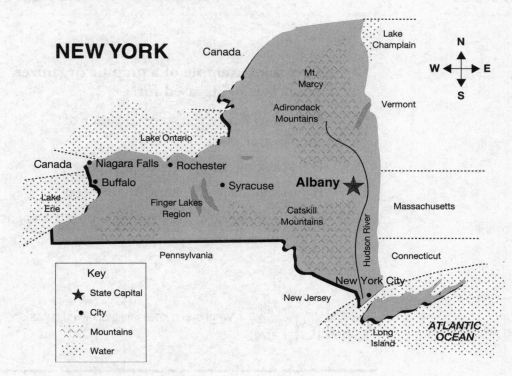

Example 1

1 **Choose the type of diagram that BEST shows a process that is always ongoing.**

A radial diagram

B cycle diagram

C organizational chart

D graphic organizer

Which type of diagram shows a circuit?

Example 2

| select number of copies | ⇒ | place paper on glass | ⇒ | press "print" | ⇒ | remove copies from tray |

2 **This is an example of a graphic organizer. What is it being used for?**

F to organize the steps in order of importance

G to show how to write a paper

H to identify the steps in a process

J to show how much time should be spent on each step

What action does this graphic organizer show?

Example 3

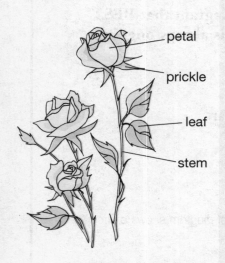

petal
prickle
leaf
stem

3 **According to this diagram, which part of the rose is found at the top of the flower?**

A leaf

B stem

C petal

D prickle

Which label is at the top of the diagram?

Test Practice

Read this article about the domesticated dog. Then answer questions 1 through 4.

General History of the Domestic Dog

Dogs are canine mammals that have been on Earth for a very long time—they have been domesticated for anywhere from 14,000 to 150,000 years. Studies of genes and fossils show that the closest animal relation to the domestic dog is the gray wolf.

Domestic dogs are common household pets, but they also perform a number of jobs for humans. Dogs can be trained to herd other animals, to hunt, to find illegal substances, and to guide humans who cannot see.

Dog Breeds

There are hundreds of breeds of domestic dogs, and they have more variation in size, appearance, and behavior than any other domestic animal. There are dogs ranging from a few inches high (the Chihuahua) to nearly three feet high (the Irish Wolfhound). They come in many different colors, too, with coats in every shade of brown, gray, and red, as well as black and white, and many patterns.

Basenji

The Basenji is an ancient dog breed native to Africa. They have been found in the tombs of Egyptian pharaohs. These extremely intelligent dogs were nearly extinct when rediscovered in the Congo region of Africa in 1895. The dogs were prized for their speed, intelligence, and courage, which made them valuable hunting dogs.

Basenji are generally quiet—they do not bark, but rather make a yodeling sound. They are generally about 17 inches high, and weigh 20 to 24 pounds. Their ears stand straight up, and they have a tightly-curled tail. They vary in color from black and white to red and white to tricolor. The breed is also known as the African Bush Dog and the African Barkless Dog.

Basenji Importation

Basenji were brought to England in the early 1900s, but disease caused them to die out. The breed was finally established there in the 1930s and soon thereafter in the United States.

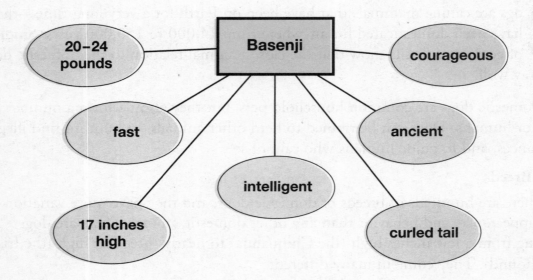

1 Under which heading would you look for information on different types of domestic dogs?

   A General History of the Domestic Dog

   B Dog Breeds

   C Basenji

   D Basenji Importation

2 In the above diagram, the **main** topic is

   F ancient

   G courageous

   H intelligent

   J Basenji

3   Read this diagram.

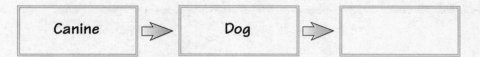

Which of the following best fills the empty box in the flow chart?

A   mammal

B   Basenji

C   Africa

D   cat

4   According to the article, which of the following happened **first**?

F   The Basenji was imported to the United States.

G   The Basenji was rediscovered in the Congo.

H   Dogs were domesticated.

J   The Basenji was imported to England.

Read this table of contents from an anthology of poetry. Then answer questions 5 through 6.

Contents

5   In which chapter of this anthology would you **most likely** find poems about animals?

A   Chapter 1

B   Chapter 2

C   Chapter 3

D   Chapter 4

6   Which chapter appears at the end of the book? How do you know this?

_____

_____

_____

CHAPTER 3

Reading Strategies and Listening Skills

Lesson 7: Context Clues

As you read, you may come across words you have not seen before. You will not always have a dictionary on hand to look up the meaning of these unfamiliar words. However, you can use the word's context to help you figure out its meaning. **Context** is what is happening in a sentence or paragraph. When you understand what is happening in the text you are reading, you can use context clues to figure out what a new word means.

Read this sentence.

> The mother was exasperated. The children kept arguing all day, even after she told them to stop.

What does "exasperated" mean? You can figure out the meaning of this word by thinking about what is happening in the sentence. You know that the children are arguing. You know that their mother is with them. How would a parent feel if her children argued all day, even after she told them to stop? She would probably feel angry and upset. That is what exasperated means. A person that is exasperated is angry and upset.

When using context clues to figure out the meaning of a word, there's an easy way to check your guess—replace the word you don't know with your guess.

 THINKING IT THROUGH Read these sentences, and then answer the question that follows.

> It was such a frigid morning. There were icicles hanging from the trees. A strong wind was blowing snow everywhere.

What does the word "frigid" mean?

_____

 HINT! Think of a word that describes the weather when there are icicles, wind, and snow. Then use that word in the sentence to see if it fits.

Example 1

"I want to write a report about how the English settlers were the first Americans," Veronica's little sister, Lucy, said.

"Okay," said Veronica. "But you're omitting something. The people from England were not the first people to live in America. You should make it clear that Native Americans lived here before settlers from outside."

Lucy said, "Oops. I guess I'll do some more research, then. I need to find out who the real first Americans were."

"Don't worry," Veronica replied. "I have some books you can peruse."

"You use big words," Lucy teased.

1a **In the story, the word "omitting" means**

A leaving out

B writing

C looking up

D thinking

1b **Which word means the same as "peruse"?**

F discuss

G enjoy

H read

I lend

Veronica tells Lucy a fact she did not include earlier.

Discuss your answer with your teacher or class.

Lesson 8
Using Prior Knowledge and Experience

P **rior knowledge** is information you already know. You learn new things every day, so your prior knowledge changes. This knowledge is not just what you have learned from books, but what you have learned from your own *experiences* as well. You may never have read or studied the effects of water on chalk, but your firsthand experience has taught you that when it rains on a chalk drawing, the drawing fades and disappears. You bring this knowledge with you when you read or write.

Prior knowledge can be thought of as the *context* you bring to anything you read. Because everyone is different, each person has a specific and unique prior knowledge. The prior knowledge of someone raised in an apartment in New York City is very different from the prior knowledge of someone raised on a dairy farm in Pamelia, New York. While both people may have the same basic education, they have different personal experiences in their lives.

You don't have to travel or do amazing things to have such knowledge—you learn many things in your everyday life. If you have siblings, you may know what younger or older kids are like. Do you live in an apartment or a house? In the city, the country, or the suburbs? What's your favorite subject in school? You have different experiences based on where you live, what your family life is like, where you go to school, what your hobbies are, what you eat, and so on.

Using your prior knowledge, you will find that even when you are reading about a topic new to you, or when reading a work of fiction you've never seen, you may already know a lot. You will be able to understand what you're reading.

Joan went up and down the rows, dropping seeds into the shallow trenches made by the hoe. As she did this, she imagined the bounty of her work: in a few months, she would taste the fruits of her labor!

How does what you have experienced give you an idea about what Joan is doing?

_____

_____

_____

 Remember that prior knowledge can come from your direct experiences or from things you have read or heard about.

If you're a gardener, it will be clear to you that Joan is planting a garden, and the "fruits" she describes are the fruits and vegetables she will grow. Even if you don't garden, you may know someone who does, or you may know a little about gardening from your reading or television. If you are reading a passage and you aren't sure about what is happening, take your time with the passage, and use your prior knowledge to help you discover the meaning.

Example 1

Yoshe helped her sister gather her bucket and shovel, and put them in the bag. They were already in their swimsuits and flipflops, and had their towels. Yoshe grabbed her sunglasses and took Yuri's hand. They walked downstairs to the kitchen, ready to go. "Mom," asked Yoshe, "do you know where the sunscreen is?"

1 **In the passage, what are Yoshe and Yuri getting ready to do?**

A   ride their bicycles

B   go to the beach

C   eat breakfast

D   go to school

Consider the details in the passage—swimsuits, towels, sunscreen—and think about what they probably mean.

Example 2

It was rush hour and Jacob was running late for work again. It was so frustrating to sit like this, just waiting to inch ahead. He wished he had bought some language tapes or some other book on tape so he at least felt like he was accomplishing something, even if it wasn't what he intended to accomplish. He inched forward, and heard the honking of horns all around him.

2 **Using what you know, you can tell that Jacob is**

F   unhappy with his job

G   riding the subway

H   dreaming

J   sitting in a traffic jam

Discuss your answer with your teacher or class.

Performance Indicators: R.1.j, R.1.n, L.1.d

Lesson 9
Making Inferences and Drawing Conclusions

Sometimes, when you read stories and passages, the writer directly tells you everything you need to know. Other times, though, you will have to figure things out for yourself. You need to make inferences or draw conclusions in order to understand the text.

An **inference** is a form of reasoning. It's an educated guess based on the information you have. For example, if a person wearing a postal uniform and carrying a bag of mail knocked on your door, you could infer that he or she was a postal carrier with a letter or package for you. Your past experience of seeing people in postal uniforms carrying mail would lead you to believe that such people are employed by the U.S. Post Office to deliver messages and packages. Because this person was knocking on your door, it would make sense that he or she was delivering something to you.

You use your own prior knowledge, as well as any other resources you have, to make inferences. When reading a nonfiction or fictional passage, you can use your prior knowledge and common sense, along with details and clues in the passage to make inferences.

Because inferences are based only on the information you have available, they can be incorrect. For example, that person at your door might be stopping only to ask directions, or could even turn out to be someone on the way to a costume party. However, the inference you make should make sense.

Remember: An inference is <u>not</u> information that is directly stated in the passage. If the author states that someone is an employee of the U.S. Post Office, you cannot infer that this is the case. The author has already told you.

Always be sure to read a passage carefully before trying to determine which choice is the proper inference. Read the passage, consider what inferences you can draw, and then look at the choices to see if any of your first impressions are there.

Example 1

The noise outside was unbearably loud. Martine was unable to concentrate on her homework. She got up and looked out of her window, feeling the afternoon breeze in her hair. Soon the noise stopped, and Martine thought about getting back to her work, but first she closed her eyes and breathed deeply the smell of freshly cut grass.

1 **From the passage, you can infer that Martine**

   A   has homework to do

   B   hears a loud noise

   C   enjoys the break from her work

   D   is on vacation

Which choice is supported by details from the passage?

Drawing Conclusions

Like inferences, conclusions should be based on the information in the passage. A **conclusion** is an overall opinion that you form after reading a passage. Inferences can lead you to a conclusion, and you can also use details and clues from the passage, prior knowledge, and your common sense. There must be evidence in the passage to support your conclusions. However, as with inferences, conclusions are not stated directly in the passage.

For example, you read that Joshua was looking forward to his music lesson. He had piano on Wednesdays after school, and wished he could have lessons on more days. He wanted to learn to play the drums and the saxophone, too. His parents said he would have to wait a few years. He could imagine himself playing the drums like Max Roach, or the saxophone like John Coltrane.

What can you conclude about Joshua from this passage? You could conclude that Joshua loves music. You could also conclude that Joshua is very determined and disciplined.

Example 2

Gerald's least favorite subject was gym. He felt like he had no control in the pool, and he didn't like the water in his eyes, his nose, or his mouth. He wore goggles and a nose clip, but whenever he was in the water, he still just flailed around, and stayed in the shallow end. The worst part was that they were moving on to basketball and soccer next month, and things would be just as bad.

2 **One conclusion you can draw from the passage is that**

F Gerald's least favorite subject was gym.

G Gerald dislikes sports.

H Gerald is a good swimmer.

J Gerald is on the swim team.

What do the clues in the passage tell you? Which choice makes the most sense based on what you read in the passage and what you know?

Lesson 10
Taking Notes

Whether you are researching a paper or preparing to answer questions on a reading passage, good note-taking skills are very useful. You will also need to take notes when you are listening to your teacher and for the English Language Arts test. You will learn more about listening in the next lesson. Read the list below for tips on how to take notes.

Note-Taking Strategies

- Do not waste time writing every word. You can leave out simple words such as *the* and *an* when you know you will not be confused by their absence.

- Take down the details that seem the most important: names of people or characters; names of places; dates; main events, and so on.

- Use your own words as much as possible when taking notes. When taking notes for a research paper, this will help you to understand the information and avoid the possibility of plagiarism—presenting someone else's words as your own.

- When you are using more than one source, use a separate page or note card for each different source, so that you can later identify where you found the information.

- Leave blank spaces between points. This allows you to locate and identify information quickly, and it also provides room to add another point you might come across.

- Leave enough room in the margins for your own additional notes.

- Write large enough and neatly enough, so that you will have no difficulty reading your own notes later.

- Know what kind of information you are looking for. While you might come across some interesting information, if it is not relevant, or connected, to your assignment, it is probably useless to you.

Now let's practice taking notes. Read the passage below, and then review the notes that follow.

Each year on the 5th of May, Mexicans remember those who fought in the Battle of Puebla in 1862, in which the Mexicans kept the French from taking control of their country. The French returned a year later, and controlled Mexico for the next five years. Mexican leader Benito Juarez led the fight to push out the French, and they left Mexico for good in 1867. Juarez became the President of Mexico, and made May a national holiday. This celebration of freedom and liberty is called Cinco de Mayo, which means "the fifth of May" in Spanish. This holiday is celebrated by Mexican-Americans in the United States as well. In the United States, the celebration focuses not on independence, but on Mexican heritage. Mexican-Americans have parties and make special, traditional meals. Some wear red, white, and green clothing, the colors of the Mexican flag.

Below is what notes for the above passage might look like:

Cinco de Mayo

Battle of Puebla, 1862, Mexicans vs. French

Benito Juarez fought against French

French leave 1867

Juarez President

Means 5th of May

Mexican-Americans celebrate heritage parties, food, Mexican colors (red, white, green)

Notice that some information from the passage does not appear in these notes, because not all the information in a passage is equally important.

Example 1

Theodore Roosevelt was the 26th President of the United States. Born in New York City in 1858, Roosevelt became well known for his adventures with the Rough Riders in the Spanish-American War. He became governor of New York in 1898, and then became Vice President under William McKinley in 1900. When McKinley was assassinated in 1901, Roosevelt became President. He was reelected, and served until 1909. He died in 1919.

1 **Write your notes based on this passage on your own paper.**

Example 2

Niagara Falls became a honeymoon destination in the 1900s, and today is a popular destination for New York visitors. More than 12 million people visit the falls each year. The falls span the border between the United States and Canada. On the U.S. side are the American Falls and Bridal Veil Fall. Horseshoe Falls is across the border in Canada. Visitors can take an elevator from Goat Island to the foot of the falls. From there, a wooden walkway takes more adventurous visitors to the falls, where they will see more than 500,000 gallons of water cascade over the cliffs each second.

2 **In this passage, it would be important to note that**

F 12 million people visit Niagara Falls each year

G Horseshoe Falls is in Canada

H Niagara Falls is popular

J The falls are near Goat Island

Discuss your answer with your teacher or class.

Performance Indicators: L.1.a-e, L.2.a-e, L.3.a-d

Lesson 11
Listening

When you take notes on a passage you are listening to, you will not be able to go back and reread the most important points. Pay careful attention when listening, and be ready to write down information as you hear it. You will not be able to answer questions correctly if your notes do not have the correct information.

Listening Skills

- Concentrate: *listening* takes more work than *hearing*.
- Watch your teacher as he or she reads the passage. Make eye contact if he or she looks up while reading.
- Listen carefully for the main points.
- Take notes on the main points.

> **Your teacher will read this article about Sandra Day O'Connor out loud to you. Read the article to yourself as your teacher reads, and take notes on your own paper as you listen. You will be asked to answer some questions at the end of the reading.**

Growing up on the Lazy B Ranch in Arizona, Sandra Day had no idea that she would someday become a role model for women the world over. Sandra Day was born in El Paso, Texas, in 1930, and grew up in Arizona. She graduated high school at age 16, and then studied economics at Stanford University in California, where she also earned her law degree. Because no California firm would hire a female lawyer in 1952, Day went into public service, becoming Deputy County Attorney for San Mateo County. That same year, she married John O'Connor. She went on to practice law in Phoenix, Arizona, and was appointed to the Arizona State Senate in 1969. In 1973, she became the first woman in the United States to serve as a state senate majority leader.

President Ronald Reagan appointed her to the Supreme Court, and she took her seat on the nation's highest court in 1981. Sandra Day O'Connor followed her own path from the Lazy B Ranch, becoming the first woman to serve on the Supreme Court.

1 **What are some important details from the article? List at least two on the lines below.**

_____

_____

_____

_____

2 **What can you conclude about Sandra Day O'Connor from the article?**

_____

_____

_____

_____

Your teacher will now read a story to you out loud. This story, a Mayan folktale about Chac, the rain god, does not appear in this book. Use your listening skills as your teacher reads, and take notes on your own paper as you listen. You will be asked to answer three questions when your teacher is finished reading.

3 List at least three important details from the story you recorded when taking notes.

_____

_____

_____

_____

4 Why does the boy keep trying to escape?

_____

_____

_____

5 Why does Chac leave the boy behind in the end?

_____

_____

_____

_____

Coached Listening

Your teacher will read you an article about the Holland Tunnel. At the end of the article, you will be asked to answer some questions. Before your teacher begins reading, review your listening and note-taking skills. Take notes on your own paper.

 Your teacher will read this selection to you.

1 List at least three important details from the article that you noted while your teacher read.

_____

_____

_____

_____

_____

2 Where is the Holland Tunnel located?

_____

_____

_____

Listening Skills

- Concentrate: listening takes more work than hearing.
- Watch your teacher as he or she reads the passage. Make eye contact if he or she looks up while reading.
- Listen carefully for the main points.
- Take notes on the main points.

3   **Why was the tunnel renamed?**

_____

_____

_____

Below is a sample answer to question number 3. This sample answer would have scored a 2, the highest score on the New York State English Language Arts test. Following the sample is a short-answer question for you to complete.

> The Holland Tunnel was named in honor of Clifford Holland. Holland was the man who decided it was a good idea to build two tunnels. He was the chief engineer on the project. He died in 1924, before the Tunnel was completed. Because of his important work on the Tunnel, it was decided to name the Tunnel after him.

4   **Why do you think Martine's answer earned the highest score?**

_____

_____

_____

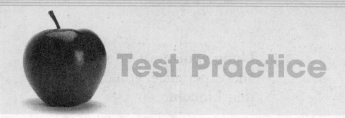

Test Practice

> **Read this article. Then answer questions 1 through 3.**

Walt Whitman was born on Long Island in New York, in 1819, the second of nine children. His family moved to Brooklyn in 1823. After only six years of school, Whitman became a printer's apprentice. After two years in his apprenticeship, he worked in a number of print shops in New York City. He also began working as a journalist, and wrote political speeches. In 1840, he worked in the presidential campaign of Martin Van Buren, and began working as a newspaper editor. While working on the *Crescent* in New Orleans, Whitman witnessed slave auctions and saw first-hand what slavery was like. These events strengthened his commitment to human rights and moved him to begin writing poetry.

In the 1840s, Whitman published a number of short stories and a novel. He published the first edition of his poetry collection *Leaves of Grass* in 1855, paying for it himself. This edition contained 12 poems. A second edition was published a year later with 20 additional poems and included a letter of congratulations from writer Ralph Waldo Emerson.

During the Civil War, one of Whitman's brothers, George, was a soldier. When George was wounded in a Virginia battle in 1862, Whitman traveled to Washington, DC. His brother was fine, but after spending time in his brother's camp, Whitman was deeply affected. He stayed on in Washington, working as a clerk for the U.S. government and visiting wounded soldiers in hospitals around the city. He was an admirer of Abraham Lincoln, and wrote a number of poems in response to Lincoln's assassination in 1865.

After the Civil War, Whitman remained in Washington, DC. By 1881, *Leaves of Grass* had been published seven times. Whitman was a famous poet. He bought a home in Camden, New Jersey, where he died in 1892.

1 From the passage, you can conclude that

  A Whitman wrote poetry

  B Whitman was opposed to slavery

  C the Civil War was fought in Virginia

  D George Whitman was killed in battle

2 From the passage it is **most** important to note that

  F Whitman worked for Martin Van Buren's presidential campaign

  G Whitman had eight siblings

  H Whitman fought in the Civil War

  J Whitman published *Leaves of Grass* in 1855

3 Using your prior knowledge and experience, you can tell that Lincoln

  A enjoyed reading poetry

  B lived in New York

  C was President of the United States

  D met Walt Whitman

Read this story. Then answer questions 4 through 6.

Miranda packed her suitcase carefully. She placed book after book in the bottom of the case. If she was going to be stuck in the middle of nowhere, she needed something suitable to read. Did they even have libraries? Cows, sure, but libraries? On top of the books, Miranda stacked her favorite clothes: blue jeans, t-shirts, sweaters, cardigans, sneakers, and two sundresses for good measure. She was done packing in a matter of minutes. After she closed the suitcase and set it next to the door of her room, she sat on the bed and looked around the room. She sighed. Two whole months away from here. Why did she have to go? Just then her mother came to the door.

"Miranda, are you ready? We have to get to the station, or we'll miss our bus." She handed Miranda her jacket. "Come on, honey."

Miranda took the jacket and glanced around the room once more before picking up her suitcase and walking out of the room behind her mother.

4 Read this sentence from the story.

> **If she was going to be stuck in the middle of nowhere, she needed something suitable to read.**

In this sentence, the word "suitable" means

F incorrect

G good

H polite

J friendly

5 Using your prior knowledge and experience, you can tell that

A Miranda is going to visit the country

B Miranda loves cows

C Miranda's mother loves the country

D Miranda packs books in her suitcase

6 What are some important details you might make note of from the passage?

_____

_____

_____

_____

CHAPTER 4

Working with Nonfiction Texts

Lesson 12: Fact and Opinion

Nonfiction is writing about facts, or events that happened. However, nonfiction can also contain opinions. A **fact** is a statement whose truth can be proven. For example, the statement "Indiana is a part of the United States" is a fact because it can be proven. By looking at a map you can see that Indiana is a state. You could also prove this by looking at books, newspapers and state documents.

An **opinion**, on the other hand, is an individual person's belief that may or may not be shared by others. For example, saying "The New York Yankees are the best baseball team ever" would be expressing an opinion, even though the team has had a great history. A person from another city might feel differently.

Opinions often involve the use of **superlatives** (words that speak in extremes), such as *all*, *everyone*, *best*, and *worst*. For example, you might write "Tina would never lie," but it would not be difficult to imagine circumstances under which Tina would lie, maybe to avoid hurting someone's feelings or to protect someone she loves. It's hard to prove that someone would *never* do something.

The same is true for **comparatives** (words that suggest a comparison), such as *better*, *nicer*, or *smarter*. What is better to one person may be worse to another.

 THINKING IT THROUGH Read the passage below, and then answer the question that follows.

Water freezes at 32° Fahrenheit.

Is this statement a fact or an opinion?

_____

 HINT! Is the statement something that can be proven or something someone believes?

Words that Often Indicate Opinions				
all	better	everyone	nobody	worst
always	best	good	none	
bad	every	never	no one	

Example 1

1 **Which statement expresses a fact?**

    A   Sharon is the prettiest girl in class.

    B   The sun provides heat and light.

    C   Nobody can run faster than I can.

    D   The Wizard of Oz was the best movie ever made.

Consider the details in the passage—swimsuits, towels, sunscreen—and think about what they indicate.

Example 2

2 **Which of the following is NOT a factual statement?**

    F   Men are always stronger than women.

    G   Dogs are usually covered with fur.

    H   Most automobiles have four wheels.

    J   Deserts are typically very hot during the day.

Discuss your answer with your teacher or class.

Lesson 13
Essential vs. Nonessential Information

In Lesson 10, you learned about finding the important information in a written passage, so that your notes included the most important information, leaving out any unimportant information. The information you recorded was **essential information**: it connected directly to your topic or to the passage. The other material in the passage—**nonessential information**—is not important to your topic or to the passage. Let's read the flyer below.

> Babysitting services available weekdays.
>
> Experienced with infants and toddlers.
>
> Kids enjoy playing together.
>
> Great play space and lunch is included.
>
> Kids like macaroni and cheese!

As you read this flyer, what do you notice? Here's a hint: If you wanted to use this babysitter, how would contact him or her? Is there a number to call? The author of this flyer has left out some essential information—the name, location, and phone number of the babysitter are important to the reader. Does the reader really need to know kids enjoy playing together? How about that kids like macaroni and cheese? This kind of information is nonessential. It serves no purpose in the flyer, and it may distract the reader from the information the author wants the reader to take from the flyer. Think about these things as you read the revised flyer on the next page.

Performance Indicators: R.1.h, R.3.a, W.1.b, L.1.b

NOTICE: Photocopying any part of this book is forbidden by law.

111

> Babysitting services available weekdays from 7 AM to 7 PM in Glenmont.
>
> Experienced with infants and toddlers.
>
> Great play space and lunch is included.
>
> Call Sue Martin: 555-3342
>
> Corner Day Care
>
> 1447 Bent Oak Drive, Glenmont

The revised flyer is much better. It has the essential information—the name, location, and number of the day care center. Now people know how to reach the babysitter.

 Read the passage below, and then answer the question that follows.

The pool has six lanes for lap swimming and 2 diving boards at the 14-foot depth. Most people enjoy diving. The entire pool was remodeled last spring, and now includes a separate kiddie pool and a sandbox and playground area. Sand is really messy. Pools hours this year are 11 AM to 9 PM daily.

What information in the passage is nonessential?

_____

_____

_____

 What information does not seem relevant to the main point of the passage?

Example 1

The Algonquin and Iroquois Indians were the first settlers of what we now call New York. More than a dozen groups of Algonquin Indians lived in what is present-day New York. Manhattan Indians lived in what is now northern Manhattan, and the Rockaways lived in Queens. Manhattan is an island. Other Indian groups included the Montauk, Munsee, Delaware, Wappinger, and Mohican. These groups lived along the coast and in the Hudson River Valley. The Iroquois lived in the inland forest areas of New York. The Canarsee lived in areas that are now Brooklyn and Staten Island. The Staten Island ferry takes commuters from Staten Island to Manhattan. The Algonquins grew maize (corn), beans, and squash. They lived in wooden houses called longhouses that held 50 or more people. They built fires inside the longhouses, which were smoky inside. Smoke isn't good for you.

1a **Which of the following information would be important information for a paper on the Algonquin Indians?**

A The Iroquois lived in the inland forest areas of New York.

B The Algonquins grew maize (corn), beans, and squash.

C Manhattan is an island.

D Smoke isn't good for you.

Which information is directly connected to the Algonquin Indians?

1b **Which of the following information from the passage can be considered nonessential?**

F "More than a dozen groups of Algonquin Indians lived in what is present-day New York."

G "Manhattan Indians lived in what is now northern Manhattan, and the Rockaways lived in Queens."

H "The Staten Island ferry takes commuters from Staten Island to Manhattan."

J "They lived in wooden houses called longhouses that held 50 or more people."

Which information is not directly related to the topic of the passage?

Example 2

The Museum of Modern Art (MoMA) is on 53rd Street in New York City. You can visit the museum any day of the week except Monday, when the museum is closed. MoMA recently reopened after a long renovation; the museum now displays much more of the artwork it used to hold in storage. The cost to view these treasures has gone up, however, and the admission price is now $20. Lots of people visit the museum. If you visit the museum often, you can get a better deal on a membership. For $75, you get unlimited entrance to the museum each year. The membership pays for itself in just four visits. The museum has a fine collection of 19th and 20th century art. Jackson Pollack was a famous painter. There is also a well-respected film and lecture series at the museum. The gift shop is also nice.

2a **Read the following sentence from the passage.**

For $75, you get unlimited entrance to the museum each year.

Why did the author most likely include this information in the passage?

A to show how expensive MoMA is

B to explain how to get to MoMA

C because MoMA was just renovated

D to explain the MoMA membership package

Does the sentence relate to the main topic of the passage?

2b **Which of the following is nonessential information from the passage?**

F "MoMA recently reopened after a long renovation; the museum now displays much more of the artwork it used to hold in storage."

G "If you visit the museum often, you can get a better deal on a membership."

H "The museum has a fine collection of 19th and 20th century art."

J "Jackson Pollack was a famous painter."

Discuss your answer with your teacher or class.

Lesson 14
Choosing the Right Texts

When you are researching your topic, you should never rely on only one source for all of your information. Why? That source might not have the most current information. It might be unreliable, or have the wrong information. It might also not provide the information you are looking for. It is usually best to use several reference sources, including:

- books—textbooks and other works of nonfiction written by experts in a field of study.

- encyclopedias—These reference sets are often the most thorough resource for research. They contain brief articles on many topics.

- articles from reputable publications—These are generally shorter works, and in recent publications, the information is very current. Before using an article as a reference, be sure that it was published by an organization that is considered reliable. For example, the *New York Times* newspaper and *Time* magazine have good reputations, but newspapers that include stories about aliens and miracle cures do not.

Taking the time to choose the rights texts pays off in the end. Your essay or report is more likely to have the correct information, and your reader will have more confidence in what you wrote.

A	B	C-Co	Cr-Cz	D-E	F-G	H-I	J-K	L	M	N	O-P	Q-R	S-Si	Sk-Sz	T-U	V-W	X-Z
1	2	3	4	5	6	7	8	9	10	11	12	13	14	15	16	17	18

Read the passage below, and then answer the question that follows.

The University of the Animal Arts has several researchers who are said to be working with talking frogs. The frogs, if they speak English, can help the researchers learn more about the animal kingdom, and can translate the language of other animals. What a benefit this will be for animal research everywhere.

Is this article from a source you can trust? Why or why not?

_____

_____

_____

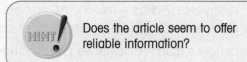 Does the article seem to offer reliable information?

Before you choose the right texts, you have to find them. Your school or public library will offer a wealth of information and sources. The easiest and most common way to find the information you are looking for is to search by topic. To search by topic, you should look up terms related to the topic you are writing about. If you were writing about dogs, for example, you might look up terms such as *dog*, *canine*, *mammal*, or *beagle*.

If you are having trouble finding information about your topic, try using more general search terms. For example, if you were not finding much information by looking up the term *beagle*, try using the more general term *dog*. Likewise, if you are finding much <u>more</u> information about a topic than you need or want, try a more <u>specific</u> search term. For example, instead of looking up *wood*, look up *mahogany*.

Remember that even the most recent books will not have the most current information on your topic. This may not matter if you are researching how thunderstorms happen, but if your topic has to do with a current science or medical issue, the information in most books will not be updated, and you may want to turn to periodicals (newspaper, magazines, and journals) in your research.

If you want to search for newspaper and magazine articles related to your topic, find out if your library has a reference book called the *Reader's Guide to Periodical Literature*. This is a publication that lists articles written about specific topics within a certain period of time, and it provides information about where and when they were published. To use the *Reader's Guide*, look up the topic in the main directory, and then go through the list of related articles. Then, using the information you found, you go through the library's collection of periodicals to find the issue you are looking for.

The key to choosing the right texts is to stay focused on your topic. Knowing what you want to write about can help you choose the best texts for your assignment and reject those sources that might be interesting but are not best suited for your needs.

Example 1

1 **Which resource should you use to find an article printed in last January's issue of *Winter Travel*?**

A standard print edition of *Encyclopaedia Britannica*

B State University of Wisconsin website

C *Reader's Guide to Periodical Literature*

D CD-ROM version of *Encyclopaedia Britannica*

Which resource would contain recent magazine articles?

New York State Coach, English Language Arts, Grade 5

Example 2

2 **You are trying to find information about jumbo jets, but your searches have not turned up many results. Which term should you try instead of *jumbo jet*?**

F airplane

G Air Force One

H helicopter

J transportation

Which term is a bit more general than "jumbo jet"?

Example 3

3 **You are researching a recent demolition and construction project in your city. Which resource would be BEST?**

A a magazine article about your city's history

B the *Encyclopedia Britannica*

C a local newspaper article on the project

D a book on construction safety

Which resource would have the most current information on your topic?

118

Coached Reading

This article is about Thai food. As you read the article, use the statements and questions in the margin to help your understanding.

Your teacher may read this selection to you.

1. Thai food is the best food you can eat. Of course, if you want to really enjoy it, you have to like spicy food,

because the best Thai food is very hot! Most people will be familiar with pad Thai, the standard noodle dish with shrimp; this dish is not usually spicy at all. Another delicious non-spicy dish is pad king, a dish made with ginger and mushrooms.

A great start for your meal is the chicken and coconut dream of a soup called tom kha gai. If you like spicy food, you might want to move on to one of the very fiery green or red curries. These are usually made with your choice of chicken, beef, or shrimp.

> Is there an opinion in this section of the passage? Can you also identify a fact?

Thai cooks create wonderful dishes with seafood. It's a specialty at most Thai restaurants. Not only shrimp, but also several varieties of fish can usually be found on the menu of many Thai restaurants. The fish may be served whole. Don't be alarmed when the plate comes to your table, and you find a fish eye staring up at you. This looks unappetizing, but the fish will be tasty (not the head). Some people don't like to eat any animal if they see the head on a plate.

Are you a vegetarian? Thai restaurants offer many vegetarian selections. Most of the standard Thai curries and pad Thai as well are available in vegetarian versions. In addition, tofu and vegetable dishes are also usually offered.

At one time you may have had to travel to a major city to locate a Thai restaurant, but these days, they can be found in most cities and suburbs of the United States. They often have fun names, such as "Thai'd Up." Look in your phone book, and head out to a Thai restaurant the next time you dine out.

Is there any nonessential information in this section of the passage?

In what type of source would you most likely find this passage?

This article is about spring in the Sonoran desert. As you read the article, use the statements and questions in the margin to help your understanding.

 Your teacher may read this selection to you.

2. Springtime in the Sonoran desert is absolutely beautiful. After a rainy winter, the desert will be awash in spectacular color. Desert plants will awaken from their sleep, and the dull colors you might expect to find will be replaced with a bounty of beautiful reds, yellows, pinks, and oranges. The earliest blooming plants will begin to show their color in February, while others may not bloom until March or April. Lots of people visit the desert in spring.

What opinion is expressed in this section of the text?

When the winter rainfall is plentiful, the spring desert will be a carpet of flowers—annuals such as poppies, lupines, and owl clover depend on rainfall. Displays of blooms through the desert from such plants occur only about once per decade, when the winter rainy season is heavier and earlier than usual. Smaller areas of the desert may have a good show of color every three to four years. Poppies are very lovely flowers.

The desert cactus will also be in bloom in spring. These plants store water, and don't need rain as much as other plants do. They will produce more blooms in a wetter year, however. The giant saguaro cactus will be dotted with yellow flowers. Photographers have taken some amazing pictures of this cactus.

What essential information is provided in this section of the passage?

Trees and large shrubs are also dependable bloomers, though blossoms will be few in drier years. Palo verdes, creosote, and whitethorn acacia all bloom in April. The spiny black sticks of the ocotillo burst open with small green leaves as soon as it rain; and in April, the plants are topped by bright red-orange spikes of flowers.

What is the likely source for this passage?

Re-read the articles, and ask yourself the questions in the margin again.
Then answer questions 1 through 5.

1 **Which of the following is a statement of opinion from article 1?**

A "Thai restaurants offer many vegetarian selections."

B "Are you a vegetarian?"

C "Thai food is the best food you can eat."

D "These are usually made with your choice of chicken, beef, or shrimp."

2 **Article 2 would be the best source for a research paper on**

F animals of the Sonoran desert

G types of flowers

H surviving in the desert

J desert plants

3 **Which of the following is a fact from article 2?**

A Poppies are very lovely flowers.

B Photographers have taken some amazing pictures of this cactus.

C The desert cactus will also be in bloom in spring.

D Springtime in the Sonoran desert is absolutely beautiful.

NOTICE: Photocopying any part of this book is forbidden by law.

123

4 **Cite two examples of nonessential information from article 2.**

_____

_____

_____

_____

5 **Article 1 is most likely from which of the following?**

F a newspaper

G the State University of New York Web site

H an encyclopedia

J a history book on Thailand

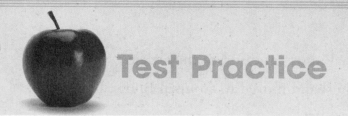

Test Practice

Read this article. Then answer questions 1 through 3.

Have you ever heard of bloomers? They were part of a fashion revolution begun by Amelia Bloomer—yes, they were named for her—in the 1850s. Bloomers were baggy pants gathered at the ankle and worn under a calf-length skirt. It doesn't seem like a revolution, but it really was. In the 1840s and 1850s, women were covered from head to toe with 8 to 16 pounds of clothing, including wire and bone corsets, hoops, petticoats, and long, heavy skirts. Such clothing was very uncomfortable and simply not practical. When Amelia's cousin Elizabeth Smith Miller came home from a trip to Europe wearing the baggy pants, Amelia loved them. She began wearing the pants and also praised them in her magazine, *The Lily*, saying, "You won't be free until you crush your corsets." A number of women followed her lead, and enjoyed the freedom of movement the new "bloomers" offered.

Amelia was born in 1818 in Homer, New York. She wanted more freedom for women in other areas of their lives. She attended the first women's rights convention, held in Seneca Falls, New York, and afterward became the first woman to publish a woman's magazine. *The Lily* included fashion tips, household advice, and information on women's rights. Women's magazines are fun reading. In 1855, Amelia and her husband moved to Council Bluffs, Iowa. Amelia Bloomer is an inspiration to us all.

1 Which of the following is essential information from the article?

A "In 1855, Amelia and her husband moved to Council Bluffs, Iowa."

B "Have you ever heard of bloomers?"

C "Women's magazines are fun reading."

D "She attended the first women's rights convention, held in Seneca Falls, New York, and afterward became the first woman to publish a woman's magazine."

2 The article is **most likely** from which source?

F a women's history periodical

G a European history textbook

H a current local newspaper

J a women's clothing magazine

3 Which of the following is **not** a statement of fact?

A "In the 1840s and 1850s, women were covered from head to toe with 8 to 16 pounds of clothing, including wire and bone corsets, hoops, petticoats, and long, heavy skirts."

B "Women's magazines are fun reading."

C "*The Lily* included fashion tips, household advice, and information on women's rights."

D "Amelia Jenks was born in 1818 in Homer, New York."

Read this article. Then answer questions 4 through 6.

The first European explorer to reach New York was Giovanni da Verrazano. The king of France hired him to explore North America, and he sailed into New York Harbor in 1524. The next explorer to reach the area was Henry Hudson, an Englishman who worked for the Dutch East India Company. Hudson was searching for a water route across North America to the pacific—what was called the Northwest Passage. The Dutch East India Company wanted a route to carry commercial goods from Asia back to Europe. Spices, silks, and jewels were traded by the company. Hudson reached New York in 1609. The company was disappointed that Hudson did not find the Northwest Passage, but claimed much of New York for the Dutch. The Dutch named the area New Netherland, and later bought the island of Manhattan from the Manhattan Indians for goods worth about $24. This was the greatest land deal the Dutch ever made. The first governor of New Netherland was Peter Minuit.

4 Which of the following is nonessential information from the article?

F "The first European explorer to reach New York was Giovanni da Verrazano."

G "The first governor of New Netherland was Peter Minuit."

H "Hudson reached New York in 1609."

J "The Dutch East India Company wanted a route to carry commercial goods from Asia back to Europe."

5   An example of **opinion** from the article is

A   "The first European explorer to reach New York was Giovanni da Verrazano."

B   "Spices, silks, and jewels were traded by the company."

C   "This was the greatest land deal the Dutch ever made."

D   "Hudson reached New York in 1609."

6   For what research topic would this article be a good source? Explain why you think so.

_____

_____

_____

_____

CHAPTER 5

Planning and Writing Constructed Responses

Lesson 15: Prewriting

The first stage in any writing project should be prewriting. **Prewriting** is what you do *before* you write. It's your chance to collect and organize your writing ideas. In the prewriting stage, you should try to come up with as many ideas as you can, and jot them down. Be creative: use everything you see around you to help you come up with ideas. You can find inspiration in books, magazines, newspapers, television, and in your own imagination: daydreaming is a great prewriting tool!

Make a list of the topic ideas you have, and then pick a few that you are really drawn to—circle these. Next, consider how an audience might respond to each idea. Your audience is likely your classmates and your teacher. Which topics would they find most interesting? Would some of the topics be more familiar to them than others? Pick the idea that seems best to you.

Once you have a topic, it's time to begin your prewriting work. There are two prewriting techniques that are especially useful: brainstorming and freewriting. This lesson will help you practice these techniques.

Brainstorming

When you **brainstorm**, you use your imagination to come up with ideas. When you brainstorm, you let ideas about the topic fly around in your mind like a whirlwind. You let your mind go where it will, and you catch the ideas and write them down in a list. The list is important—if you don't write your ideas down, you may forget some of them. You don't have to worry about spelling, and you don't have to write your ideas out in complete sentences. Brainstorming will bring a flurry of ideas to you, and you don't want to slow down and think too much. Just jot down enough information so that you will remember the idea when you look back at the list. The ideas you come up with while brainstorming will give you a place to start writing. Let's look at an example of how brainstorming works.

Martine has been asked to write an essay on her favorite subject in school. Since she loves science, this is what Martine decides to write about. To begin brainstorming, Martine starts with a blank piece of paper. She writes "Why science is my favorite subject" at the top. Then she takes a deep breath, picks up her pen and begins to write down everything that comes into her mind when she thinks about science. The results of her brainstorm are below.

Why science is my favorite subject

- I'm good at science
- It's fun
- experiments
- cool equipment
- great teachers
- solving problems
- discovering new things
- Albert Einstein
- science fair

 Reread Martine's list, and then answer the question below.

What do you notice about Martine's list?

_____

_____

_____

 Does Martine write in complete sentences? What kinds of things are on her list?

Freewriting

Freewriting is another form of prewriting that gets your creative juices flowing. Freewriting starts you thinking about your topic and gives you a chance to jot down whatever you think about it. To freewrite, you let your ideas flow, writing down anything that you think of, no matter how silly or unrelated to your topic it may seem. You usually give yourself a set amount of time, such as one minute, and you don't stop writing until your time is up. As in brainstorming, you don't need to worry about using complete sentences or punctuation. Let's look at an example of how freewriting works.

Martine decides to freewrite for one minute about why she likes science. To begin this exercise, she first writes "Why science is my favorite subject" at the top of her blank sheet of paper. She sets a timer for one minute. Then she picks up her pen and writes down whatever comes into her mind when she thinks of science.

Why science is my favorite subject

Science is my favorite subject because I'm really good at it and it's fun. I love my science teacher. Experiments! Always did experiments. In the kitchen. In the yard, with dirt and rocks. Like working things out. Doing things on my own. Feels good to know things. See science everywhere I look. The desk, the tree outside. All science. Be a researcher. Or doctor.

When working on your own writing projects, you can use one or both of these exercises to get you started. Below is a list of topics. Choose the one that you like best. You will use it for your brainstorming and freewriting exercises.

Possible topics:

- My favorite subject
- Why my room is special
- My favorite vacation
- How I learned to ride a bike
- What I love to do on a rainy day
- The last book I read
- My hobby
- A day I'll always remember

Example 1

Now it's your turn to try brainstorming. Write the topic you selected in the space below. *Make sure you have selected a topic you really like, because you will be working with it throughout this chapter.* Now brainstorm ideas about your topic and write them on the lines that follow.

Brainstorm Exercise:

My topic is: _____

_____

_____

_____

_____

_____

_____

_____

_____

_____

_____

_____

_____

_____

_____

Example 2

Now it's your turn to try freewriting. Begin with the same topic you picked for the brainstorming exercise in Example 1. Give yourself a set amount of time—try 1 minute. Then freewrite ideas about your topic on the lines that follow.

Freewriting Exercise:

My topic is: _____

_____

_____

_____

_____

_____

_____

_____

_____

_____

_____

_____

_____

_____

Performance Indicators: W.1.b, W.1.f, W.1.g, W.3.a, W.3.f, W.CPI.5

Lesson 16
Outlining and Drafting

Now that you've done your prewriting exercises, you are ready to really start planning your writing. Before you start to write, you should know what it is you are going to write about. Take the ideas you came up with in prewriting, and organize them into the shape of your paper. After you organize your ideas, you will be ready to start writing paragraphs. The next steps in the writing process are outlining and drafting.

Outlining

An outline acts as a frame for your writing. To create an outline, you take the ideas you had in prewriting, and identify the main topics you will discuss in your paper. List these main topics in the order you will write about them, and number them using Roman numerals. Jamar is writing a paper about Mount Rushmore. The main topics he has chosen are below.

    I.   Why monument was built

    II. Building the monument

    III. Completed monument

After you list the main topics, go back and fill in supporting information under each main topic. Think of each of the main topics as a paragraph, and identify the supporting information you will write in each one. Place this information below the main topic in the outline, and label each separate piece of information with capital letters. Look at Jamar's outline on the next page.

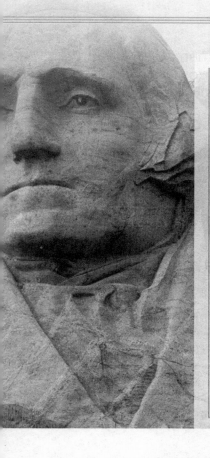

I.   Why monument was built
    A. wealth and tourism
    B. a tourist site in South Dakota
    C. a monument to U.S. leaders

II. Building the monument
    A. a sculptor's dream
    B. carving a mountain
    C. the Great Depression
    D. public works project

III. Completed monument
    A. October 1941
    B. Dedications

Jamar's outline gives him a basic plan for his essay. Looking at the outline, Jamar can get a clearer idea of the main idea of his passage. Once he does this, he will create a **thesis statement**, which is a sentence that gives readers the main idea and structure of an essay. It includes the main idea of the passage. When he begins to write, Jamar will place his thesis statement in the first paragraph of his essay (usually at the end of the paragraph). This first paragraph is called the **introduction**, or introductory paragraph. He will use this paragraph to tell his readers what his essay will be about. He will then follow his outline, writing **supporting paragraphs**—paragraphs that support his thesis statement with facts and details. Each paragraph in Jamar's essay should help develop his thesis statement and convince his readers that it's true. For example, under the main topic "Building the monument," Jamar lists four separate pieces of information: a sculptor's dream; carving a mountain; the Great Depression; and public works project. These will become details in the paragraph. By writing an outline, Jamar has planned what each paragraph will be about. At the end of his essay, Jamar will write a **conclusion**, a short paragraph that summarizes his essay and reminds readers of his thesis statement.

Writing an outline keeps you organized and focused. You can tell before you write your essay if you are repeating ideas or if you need to change the order in which you present them. Changing things in an outline is easier than having to change things <u>after</u> you have written the first draft of your essay.

A graphic organizer is another way to plan your writing. As you remember, we discussed organizers in Lesson 6. Instead of a list, you could use boxes and connecting lines. Your first point goes in the first box, your second point goes in the second box, and so on. The arrows help you remember the order you should follow. A graphic organizer based on part of Jamar's outline is below.

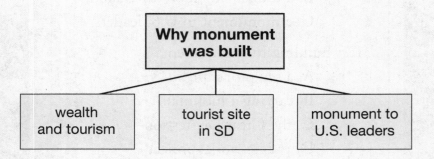

Notice that the bigger box states the paragraph's main idea. The details that Jamar will include in this paragraph are in the smaller boxes.

Example 1

> Now look at your topic and prewriting exercises from the previous lesson. On your own paper, create an outline for your topic. First, figure out what your main idea is and write a thesis statement. Then include at least two supporting paragraphs in your outline and three details for each paragraph. Use Roman numerals to list the topic of each supporting paragraph.
>
> Once you have completed your outline, use it to create a graphic organizer for your topic.
>
>
>
> Use your freewriting exercise to help you fill in your outline.

Drafting

After outlining, the next step in the writing process is drafting. The purpose of drafting is to get words down onto paper. You've might have heard the phrase "rough draft" before. A draft is not what your final essay will look like, but it's a step to getting there.

For your draft, you will use your prewriting notes, as well as your outline and graphic organizer, to remind you of what you want to say in the essay. You will begin your paper with an introductory paragraph that explains your essay topic and gets the reader's attention.

The paper's introduction should state what the paper is about, but without giving too much detail. It should leave your reader with a clear sense of the organization and goal of your essay. For example, the introduction to Jamar's paper about Mount Rushmore might read as follows:

> Who would have thought that carving four giant faces into a mountain would be possible? Mount Rushmore shows how creativity and determination can make great things happen. The monument is also a lasting record of a time when the United States seemed to have a great deal of ambition and confidence. Mount Rushmore is a record of a sculptor's dream and of a special time in America's history.

Your introductory paragraph might be longer or shorter than this. Remember that you want your introduction to:

- interest your reader in the essay
- set the stage for what the paper will be about
- give the reader an idea of the paper's organization

First, try to get the reader interested in your topic. To do this, think about why you are interested in your topic, then tell that to your reader. Next, tell the reader what shape the essay will take. Why? Readers like to know what to expect as they read. It helps them follow the points you're making as you make them. Try *not* to say, "First, I'll talk about creativity and determination. Then I'll talk about the time period." This is boring and draws too much attention to your role as the writer. Finally, state the main idea of your essay in a thesis statement.

Reread Jamar's introductory paragraph, and then answer the question below.

Who would have thought that carving four giant faces into a mountain would be possible? Mount Rushmore shows how creativity and determination can make great things happen. The monument is also a lasting record of a time when the United States seemed to have a great deal of ambition and confidence. Mount Rushmore is a record of a sculptor's dream and of a special time in America's history.

What is Jamar's thesis statement?

_____

_____

_____

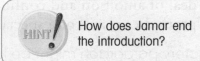 How does Jamar end the introduction?

Example 2

Now it's your turn to try drafting. In the space below, write an introduction to the essay topic you outlined earlier in this lesson. Be sure to include a thesis statement. Use your own paper if you need more space.

_____

_____

_____

_____

Lesson 17
Organizing Your Response

You now know your topic and have outlined the structure of your essay. You've even written an introductory paragraph. Before you begin the rest of your essay, stop and think about your paper for a moment. Consider your main idea and the supporting paragraphs of your outline. What might be the best way to present this information?

In Chapter 2, you learned about ways texts are structured. When writing your own texts, you will need to choose an organizational method. The information in your outline should help you determine the best way to organize your essay. There are a number of choices. In some cases, sequence, or order of events (see Lesson 5) may be the best choice. You may also want to use the general to specific method of organization, the cause and effect method, or comparison and contrast. These are discussed in this lesson.

General to Specific

You may want to begin your essay by writing about your topic in general, then narrowing it down to make it more specific. For example, read the following paragraph:

> There are many types of transportation available in most U.S. cities. You could certainly take your car, but if you do, try to carpool to save energy. Even better than this is public transportation. Look into the kinds of public transportation available in your neighborhood. Even if you aren't close to a subway station, chances are that there is a bus stop near your home. Buses run frequently, and stop in most neighborhoods. They are less expensive than the cost of owning, driving, and maintaining your own car, and they are much friendlier to the environment.

As you're reading, what's something you notice about this paragraph? Think about how the paragraph starts. In the beginning, it's very general. By the end, though, the topic has been narrowed down a great deal.

Let's look at a graphic organizer of the information in this passage:

As you can see, the most general topic of the paragraph—transportation—is at the far left of the diagram. It's also at the beginning of the paragraph. Similarly, the most specific item—buses—is at the far right of the diagram and at the end of the paragraph.

Cause and Effect

The cause-and-effect method of organizing an essay shows readers the relationships between things. The cause is the action or event, and the effect is what happens as a result of the event or action. Basically, this means that when you read about something important that happens in a passage, you know why it happened because the writer told you about the events that led up to it. For example, "The sun was hot, and my ice cream melted." In this sentence, the cause is the hot sun, and the effect is that the ice cream melted. A diagram of the cause and effect is below.

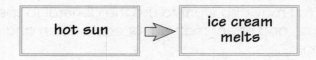

The cause-and-effect method is used to
- explain a process
- identify the reasons why an event happened
- point out the actual or possible results of situations or actions

Read the passage below, and then answer the question that follows.

Marianne turned on the water to run a bath, and then ran downstairs to answer the phone. She chatted with her friend Marcy for about a half hour, and was reminded of her bath when she saw water running down the steps.

What is the cause-and-effect relationship in this passage?

_____

_____

_____

_____

_____

_____

 HINT! What happens in the passage? Does something cause this to happen?

Words Used in Cause-and-Effect Writing

- so
- because
- as a result
- since
- therefore
- then

Comparison and Contrast

Like cause and effect, comparison and contrast also shows readers the relationships between things. Comparison shows how things are alike, or similar. For example, if you were writing about cars and buses, you could say that both of them are forms of transportation, and both have wheels. Contrast, on the other hand, shows how things are different. You could say that cars are used by individuals, and buses are used in public transportation systems. This structure is useful when you are writing about two or more things. To use this structure in your essay, you need to—

- Identify how the two or more things are similar and how they are different.
- Decide on your focus—will you mainly stress the differences, the similarities, or try to strike a balance?

Words That Show Similarities					
like	same	both	as well as	similarity	as
in the same way	have in common	most important	the same as	similar	too

Words That Show Differences						
although	whereas	however	unlike	unless	even though	yet
but	instead	while	on the contrary	on the other hand	contrary to	the reverse

A Venn diagram can be very useful in showing the similarities and differences between two things.

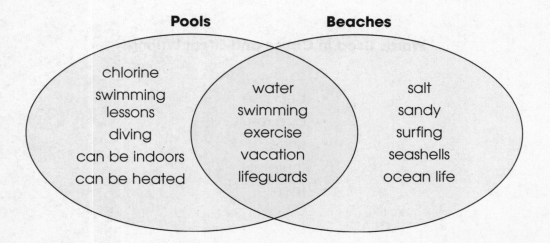

Pools — Beaches

Pools: chlorine, swimming lessons, diving, can be indoors, can be heated

Both: water, swimming, exercise, vacation, lifeguards

Beaches: salt, sandy, surfing, seashells, ocean life

The diagram on page 142 expresses the similarities and differences between a beach and a pool. The qualities that these two things share is in the overlapping portion of the circles, the section in the middle. The information in each circle, but not in the overlapping portion, is what is different between a beach and a pool.

 THINKING IT THROUGH Look again at the Venn diagram on page 142, then answer the question that follows.

Name two similarities and two differences between a pool and a beach, according to the diagram.

_____

_____

_____

 HINT! Look at the overlapping section of the diagram, as well as the individual sections of each circle.

Example 1

Ariel went camping every June with her cousins. Last summer was one to remember. She was rock climbing with them, when she lost her grip and tumbled several feet to the ground. Her cousins tried to help her back to camp, but in the end, one of them went back and contacted the ranger's office. Ariel had to be carried out of the park on a stretcher and taken to the hospital. She broke her ankle, which was the end of that year's camping trip for her.

1 **Which organizational method does this passage use?**

A organization

B cause and effect

C general to specific

D compare and contrast

Does the passage compare two things? Does it illustrate an event caused by another event?

Example 2

Yoshe loved to play soccer, and in fact, she would say it was her favorite sport. She liked other sports. Basketball was another favorite, but it was played inside, while soccer was played outside. Yoshe really enjoyed being outdoors—it was part of why she was so athletic. Basketball involved dribbling, passing the ball with your hands, and scoring that way as well. She wasn't really sure why, but Yoshe was much more comfortable passing the ball—and scoring—with her feet. This made soccer the perfect game for her.

2 **This passage uses which of the following organizational methods?**

F sequence

G cause and effect

H general to specific

J compare and contrast

Does the passage begin with a general idea and move on to a specific one? Does it compare and contrast two things?

Writing Practice

Now you are ready to draft your essay. Look back at the outline and introductory paragraph you created in Lesson 16. Then decide which organizational method you will use in your essay. Is there anything you want to change in your outline or your introduction? Consider this now, and make any changes before you begin to write. In the space below, draft your essay. Your essay should include:

- An introduction with a thesis statement
- At least 2 supporting paragraphs
- A conclusion

Performance Indicators: W.1.c, W.1.g, W.3.b

Lesson 18
Topic Sentences and Supporting Details

With a good thesis statement, it should be pretty clear what to do next: start writing the paragraphs that support your statement. For each paragraph, first state the topic of the paragraph, and then include specific examples or information.

The main idea of each of your supporting paragraphs will be stated in a topic sentence. The **topic sentence** is the sentence that expresses the main idea of the paragraph. It establishes what the paragraph is about, and all other sentences in the paragraph directly relate back to it. It is most often found at or near the beginning of the paragraph.

 Read this passage, then answer the question that follows.

One of the main ways that you can stay safe on the road is to wear a seatbelt. Some people get into their cars and don't bother putting on their seatbelts. They are putting their lives at risk. There are thousands of car accidents every day throughout the country. Seatbelts can keep riders more secure in their seats and prevent serious injury.

What is the main idea of this passage?

_____

_____

_____

_____

 Reread the passage and identify its topic sentence.

NOTICE: Photocopying any part of this book is forbidden by law.

Writing a topic sentence is the first step in writing a supporting paragraph. Once you know the topic sentence, you must work on adding facts, details, and examples that back up your topic sentence. You want to include information in the paragraph that will convince the reader that your overall thesis and the topic sentence of your paragraph are believable and correct.

If you aren't sure what information you should add to your paragraph, look at your outline. You included main topics for paragraphs and supporting details on the outline. What information did you include for your first supporting paragraph?

If you're still having trouble figuring out what to write, try another brainstorming exercise. At the top of a blank sheet of paper, write the main topic of your first supporting paragraph. Turn this topic into a topic sentence, and beneath this sentence, write everything you can think of related to this topic sentence.

Once you have another list for reference, remember that you don't have to include everything on your list in the paragraph. In fact, it's a good idea to go through your list and pick a few examples that will best illustrate your topic sentence. Perhaps you have some facts, an example, or a story from your own life that you can use to make your point clear to the reader. Review the details you have chosen and make sure that they are relevant. In other words, your details should be directly connected to the topic sentence. Remove any details that aren't relevant before you write your paragraph.

Example 1

Education is very important. Today's students will find it harder than ever to successfully enter the job market without at least a high school diploma. In many cases, a college degree is required. Most people like school. It's important that government continue to spend tax dollars on public education so that today's students can become tomorrow's workers.

1a **What is the topic sentence of this paragraph?**

_____

_____

_____

_____

_____

_____

_____

Which sentence tells the reader what the paragraph will be about?

1b **Which sentence from the paragraph does not belong there?**

A "Education is very important."

B "Today's students will find it harder than ever to successfully enter the job market without at least a high school diploma."

C "Most people like school."

D "In many cases, a college degree is required."

Discuss your answer with your teacher or class.

Let's look at a supporting paragraph from Jamar's essay on Mount Rushmore:

> The building of Mt. Rushmore was partly the result of this country's confidence and wealth. After World War I, the U.S. enjoyed a period of wealth and growth. More families had the income to buy an automobile and the free time to travel. Doane Robinson, the state historian of South Dakota, had a plan to bring these tourists to his state. Inspired by the towering rock formations of the Black Hills, Robinson wrote to a famous sculptor in 1924. He proposed that a group of giant sculptures be carved into the mountains. The artist had a better idea. He convinced Robinson and the state's political leaders that the sculpture should be a monument to America's greatest leaders.

Jamar's paragraph begins with a topic sentence and is followed by supporting information about the changes in the U.S. that contributed to the building of Mt. Rushmore.

Now look back at your <u>first</u> supporting paragraph from the Writing Practice on page 145. Does your paragraph begin with a clear topic sentence? Can you add more details to your paragraph to support and illustrate your topic sentence?

In the space below, rewrite this supporting paragraph using what you have learned in this lesson.

Lesson 19
Developing Your Essay

You now have the tools you need to write a complete draft of an essay. To practice those skills, read the paragraph in Example 1.

Example 1

Going to amusement parks is really a fun way to spend your vacation. You can ride the rides, and it's really fun. Try an amusement park.

This paragraph is a first draft. Although it begins with a topic sentence, the topic is poorly developed. This means the paragraph lacks the details to support its topic sentence and make it interesting and believable for the reader. Revise the paragraph on your own paper, developing it by adding supporting details, examples, facts, or anecdotes (a story about something that happened to you).

What kind of information will help support the topic sentence?

Now look back again to the Writing Practice on page 145. This time, reread your <u>second</u> supporting paragraph. On the lines below, revise the second paragraph from your essay. When revising, make sure that your paragraph includes a clear topic sentence and supporting details that help prove your topic sentence.

Lesson 20
Editing and Revising

Nobody is perfect, especially when it comes to writing. Generally speaking, when you write, you are not writing a final draft right away. In the first attempt you make to write a paper, your goal is to list the information you want to provide and to say what you want to say. Because you are focusing on getting the information in writing, you are likely to make errors in spelling, grammar, and punctuation. It is also common for a first draft to include errors in clarity, meaning that what you have written is not exactly what you intended to say. After you have finished your first draft, you need to edit and revise it.

Give yourself plenty of time to write and revise your essay. After you have written a first draft, take a break from your writing before you begin to edit and revise. That way you'll have a fresh perspective on the text. If you have a few days, great—if you have only a few minutes, that's fine, too. Take whatever time you have and step away from your essay. Do something else, or think about something else.

When you go back to your essay after a break, read very slowly and carefully, considering each sentence. Reading quickly may lead you to miss errors. If you can, you should read your paper out loud. Sometimes you will hear things that your eyes missed.

It can also be helpful to have someone else read your paper. They will often catch errors and problems you do not. Do not simply rely on the spellcheck tool on your computer (if you use one). While useful, this tool will not catch all errors in spelling or usage.

You should look for very specific errors at the sentence level (punctuation, grammar). Also review the more general elements of your paper as covered in this chapter:

- Do you have a thesis statement and topic sentences for your paragraphs?
- Does your essay have an introduction?
- Did you choose a useful method of organization for your information?
- Are your paragraphs well supported with facts, examples, etc.?
- Do your supporting paragraphs prove your thesis statement?
- Does your paper include a conclusion that wraps everything up, restates (but does not simply *repeat*) your major points, and put your argument in perspective?

Editing and revising is an important step in writing. It gives you the chance to add details and catch errors that might be distracting to the reader, making your essay more convincing and effective. When you proofread your paper, you reread what you have written, and you look for specific types of errors. After you finish the first draft of your essay, read through the editing checklist below and then check your paper. These reminders will help you identify errors in your writing.

Editing Checklist

1 Check your capitalization and punctuation.

2 Spell all words correctly.

3 Check for sentence fragments or run-on sentences.

4 Keep verb tense consistent.

5 Make sure subjects and verbs agree.

6 Use words according to the rules of Standard English.

7 Remember to paragraph correctly.

Example 1

It took more than too years to raise the money and develop the techniques needed to carve the mountain. In October of 1927, a crew climbing a forty-story staircase and began to shape the rock's face with jackhammers, rock drills, and dynamight. Two years later, in 1929, the stock market crashes and America enterd the Great Depreshion. The monument to america's greatness became one of the greatest public works projects ever it was funded by the federal government to provide jobs in South Dakota.

---

1 **Use the Editing Checklist on page 154 to review this paragraph. Correct any errors and rewrite the paragraph in the space below.**

Discuss your answer with your teacher or class.

NOTICE: Photocopying any part of this book is forbidden by law.

155

Writing Practice

It's now time to write the final version of the essay you have been working on throughout this chapter. Use the editing and revising tips you learned in Lesson 20 as you re-read and review what you have written so far, and then write a final version on the lines that follow. Your final version should include a conclusion. This is a final paragraph that—

- Restates your thesis statement (though it should not only repeat your thesis statement)
- Summarizes the ideas you presented in your supporting paragraphs (your topic sentences)
- Leaves the reader with something new to think about.

After you've completed your final draft, use the Editing Checklist from Lesson 20 to look for any errors. If you need to make corrections in the final version, be sure to make them neatly.

Performance Indicators: R.3.a, R.3.b, R.3.c, W.3.c, W.3.d, W.3.e, L.3.a, L.3.b, L.3.c, L.3.d

CHAPTER 6 — Reading Persuasive Texts

Lesson 21: Elements of a Good Argument

When you hear the word *argument*, you might think of a disagreement. In writing, however, **argument** refers to the author's position on a topic, how he or she feels about it, and why the author has taken this position. The author might state his or her position, or perspective, clearly in the text. This is generally the case with **editorials** and letters to the editor. The author of such a text will have an opinion on the topic, and the author's goal is to persuade the reader to agree with that opinion.

To be persuasive, it's not enough for the writer to express his or her position and leave it at that. A good argument has two parts:

- a statement of the author's position
- the reasons why the reader should agree with the author's position

The first sentence of an editorial about library hours might read as follows:

> Public libraries need more funding to help them stay open during the hours when schoolchildren need them most.

You can tell from this statement that the author believes that public libraries need to be open for longer hours. Is this statement by itself an argument? No—it tells the reader the author's viewpoint, but it does not give reasons why the author believes this, or why the reader should agree with him. What might the author's reasons be for his point of view? He will have to explain why it's important to give libraries more funding and maintain their hours.

Read the passage below, and then answer the question that follows.

To the Editor:

Public libraries need more funding to help them stay open during the hours when schoolchildren need them most. Libraries are cutting back on their hours in the middle of the school year, when most school-aged children have the greatest need for the library's services. Most people believe in education for children, or at least they say that they do. It's time to put our money where our mouths are, and demand that the City Council finds the funds necessary to keep the libraries open.

Does the author present a convincing argument for his viewpoint?

_____

_____

_____

 Does the author of this editorial give reasons why the reader should agree with his viewpoint?

It's important, when making an argument, to lay out your position well. When arguments are clearly presented, they usually win more supporters. That's really the point of making an argument.

The author uses the reasons for his position to convince the reader of his argument. In an argument, certain kinds of reasons work well. A really good argument will not only present the writer's viewpoint, but will also address the reader's concerns. This means the author should not only give reasons for his or her position; the author should also respond to whatever objections readers might have. Objections are reasons why the reader would <u>not</u> agree with the author's argument. The author should create an argument convincing enough to sway these readers. Does that sound complicated? It's really not.

Let's consider the editorial on public libraries on the previous page. What objections to the author's viewpoint might a reader have? A concern might be the funding. Where will the money come from to keep the libraries open? The editorial is below again, and this time, the author has addressed this possible concern.

> Public libraries need more funding to help them stay open during the hours when schoolchildren need them most. Libraries are cutting back on their hours in the middle of the school year, when most school-aged children have the greatest need for the library's services. Most people believe in education for children, or at least say that they do. It's time to put our money where our mouths are, and demand that the city council find the funds necessary to keep the libraries open. The funds are there. There's money left over from the local road repair division and from the election planning fund. These could be tapped into without requiring that the state go into debt or deny another agency its necessary funding.

To find convincing reasons for an argument, think about the topic in general. What makes longer library hours a good idea? As mentioned in this editorial, students use the library after school. Can you think of any other reasons why longer library hours are a good idea? What about working adults? They might need to use the library in the evenings, as well.

In writing an editorial, your argument will be more persuasive if it presented in a clear and concise manner. A concise argument gets to the point without adding unnecessary details. The author's viewpoint and the reasons for it should be clear to the reader.

Dear Editor,

The downtown space near the old movie theater is vacant and an eyesore. If the city wants to, they could make good use of it. One thing they could do is make it into a public park. People also love gardens. A place for people to walk their dogs or go strolling after work would be great for families. I love parks. My aunt has a beautiful garden in her backyard. Someone would have to clean up the lot and remove all of the garbage. Maybe the public works department could do this. People who go to the movie theater don't like the lot.

Does this editorial have a convincing argument? It's difficult to say, after reading the editorial, what the author's argument is, and it's not very persuasive. The author drifts around her point and includes a lot of unnecessary information. Let's look at this editorial again, as rewritten to make its argument clear and concise. The revised editorial begins with a clear statement of the author's position.

Dear Editor,

The vacant lot downtown next to the old movie theater should be turned into a public park space featuring gardens. The lot is an eyesore and regularly fills with garbage. By cleaning up the space, our city could provide a place for local residents to enjoy nature and to garden. The city owns the lot, and has no current plans for it. The cleanup of the lot could be done by local residents with materials provided by the public works department. Some people are worried about the cost. The department would have no labor costs, and other expenses would be very small: dirt, stones for pathways, perhaps several benches, and some fencing for the garden area. The lot is not very large. Materials required would be less than the public works department normally uses for the west side park each spring, and not much more than they regularly spend to clean up the garbage in the lot.

How does the editorial read now? The author's argument is clearly stated right up front. The reasons for the author's viewpoint are expressed, including some responses to possible arguments from those opposed to the idea.

The editorials we've seen in this lesson give reasons for doing or thinking something—positive arguments. These are usually the most convincing when making an argument, but you can also point out the effects of *not* doing or thinking something. These are called negative arguments. In the example of the vacant lot, for example, you could use the negative argument that not turning the lot into a park space would result in continued garbage piling up there, which would create a damaging effect on the rest of the neighborhood. Try not to spend too much time on the negative, because that focuses your reader's attention in the wrong place.

When you're forming an argument, what you're trying to do is convince your reader to feel the way you do. Hard evidence, or proof—such as studies and statistics—might convince your readers that your position is the right one. They might agree that it makes sense. But that might not be enough to convince them. If you make your readers care about your issue—by appealing to their emotions—you'll probably convince them. Combining evidence and emotion can lead to a strong argument.

Example 1

The farmer's market in Wakefield Park should be maintained. The market has been around for three decades, and gives urban residents the opportunity to buy produce and plants directly from the growers. As someone raising children in the city, I can tell you that the farmer's market gives kids the chance to see that food does not just come from a grocery store. They can talk with farmers and discover what life outside the city is like. The market has marked the beginning and end of the summer season for as long as I can remember. Residents come from throughout the city to make their purchases each week. The city wants to increase the farmers' lease on the space to such a degree that they will not be able to afford to stay. This is inexcusable. Keep the farmers in the city!

1 **What is the author's point of view in this editorial?**

A Kids love the farmer's market.

B The farmer's market in Wakefield Park should be kept.

C Farmers belong in the city.

D Vegetables are good for you.

What is the author trying to convince the reader of?

Example 2

1. The new tax on groceries has got to go. It's clear that the state has budget issues, but a tax on groceries hurts those who can least afford it—the middle and lower-income families who are already struggling to get by. Such people may already buy only the necessities, doing without luxuries such as dining out and purchasing new cars. Now they are faced with a tax on the one necessity they cannot do without. Do we really want to force a family to choose between milk and bread in the grocery store because the tax will not let them afford both? Grocery stores will feel the pinch of this tax, as well, in the form of reduced sales. The governor must find other ways to raise the money needed for her budget. What about an increased tax on true luxuries, such as expensive cars or houses?

2. If we want to keep Westwood Elementary School open, we should do something. Does anyone send their child to this school? Once it was a family place, but the neighborhood has changed. Are there fewer kids in the neighborhood? It doesn't seem like it. But why else would they close the school? Where will the neighborhood kids go now? They should put more money into the school.

2 **Which of these editorials is more effective? Explain why you think so, and what you would do to make the other editorial more convincing to the reader. Use your own paper.**

Discuss your answer with your teacher or class.

Lesson 22
Book and Movie Reviews

Writing a review is a lot like writing an editorial, which you learned about in the last lesson. A **review** is a nonfiction article evaluating a book, play, movie, restaurant, concert, or other event. In this chapter, we will focus on book and movie reviews.

You may have read a review before, and it's likely that you have written them as well. Have you ever written an essay about your favorite book? In essence, this was a book review. When reviewing a book or movie, authors present their opinion of the book, or their viewpoint. They then back up their opinion with information and facts from the book or movie.

To help you write a good review, you will need to use your note-taking skills and record the important information from the book or movie you are reviewing, as well as your impressions of it. You may have ideas about what you want to write while you are reading (or watching), so have a pencil and paper nearby. Let's use a book for our first example.

The first thing you should include in your review is information on the type of book you are reviewing: is it fiction, nonfiction, or poetry? You should also provide the book's title and the author's name right up front in your review. It can be very frustrating to read a review for paragraphs without knowing what is being reviewed. To avoid frustrating or distracting your reader in this way, always place that information at the beginning of your review, in the first few sentences or the first paragraph.

If you thought the book had a theme, you might include that early on as well. You will learn more about theme in Lesson 34. Next, provide the reader with a brief summary of the book. Tell its main thesis and supporting points, if the book is nonfiction. For fiction, review the characters, setting, and plot, but do not reveal any information that readers might not wish to know should they read the book themselves. Don't give away any plot twists or secrets. You can include quotes from the book if you like, to give the reader a better idea of the writer's style, but this is not necessary.

Now you are ready to share your opinion of the book with your reader. As with an editorial or other persuasive writing, it will not be enough for you to only state your opinion. You will need to provide the reader with the *reasons* for this opinion. Many of these questions would apply to movie reviews as well. Questions to ask yourself and answer for the reader include:

- Did I find the book interesting?
- If the book was nonfiction, was I convinced by its argument?
- Were there problems with the argument presented in the book?
- Did I agree with the argument?
- Did the book interest me?
- Did I find the characters realistic?
- Did the plot work well?
- Was anything missing from the story?
- Did the book conclude well?
- How does the book compare to something else I have read?
- Did the book change the way I look at the world?
- How did the book affect me?
- Did the book bring up any issues that I want to present to my readers?

After you have related your own opinions, you are ready to conclude your review with a brief summary of your ideas and opinions about the book. You may also want to advise the reader to read the book (or not).

Let's look at two reviews of the same book. Yoshe and Kavi both had to read *Little Women* for their English class. They both read the book and wrote the reviews on the next page. As you will see, they felt differently about the book. First let's look at Yoshe's review.

The book <u>Little Women</u>, by Louisa May Alcott, is fiction, although it's based on Alcott's life. The story is mainly about Jo March. Jo has three sisters: Meg, Beth, and Amy. The book shows the four of them and their life together in New England. They are poor, but happy. I thought Jo was really inspiring, because she wants to be a writer and doesn't always like to do what girls were expected to do then. She does what she wants to do, and in the end, she is successful. This gives me hope for my own future in sports. The sisters have real relationships, and they fight and make up like sisters do. The reader always knows that they love each other. One of the sister dies, which is very sad, but the novel ends well. I highly recommend the book for anyone who wants an interesting and inspiring book to read.

Yoshe really seemed to like the book. She includes the important information in her review, and tells us why the book was meaningful for her. In the end, she recommends the book to her readers. She gives away the fact that one of the sisters dies, but doesn't say which one, and this might actually make the reader interested in the book. Now let's look at Kavi's review.

I read the book <u>Little Women</u> for English class. The story is by Louisa May Alcott, and it takes place in New England around the time of the Civil War. The March family is struggling to live, because the father is away helping with the northern side of the war. The reader doesn't get much information on the Civil War, which happens far away. I found this disappointing. The book is about four sisters named Meg, Jo, Beth, and Amy. They are all very different but get along well, and each one tries to help the family through difficult times. There is a neighbor named Laurie (a boy!) who is wealthy and becomes their friend. They have adventures and do family things, and the book ends with Jo getting married. Because its mostly about sisters, I think girls would like the book better than I did. I would rather read a nonfiction book about the Civil War.

Kavi's reaction to the book was different from Yoshe's. He didn't dislike it, exactly, but he also didn't feel inspired by it as Yoshe did. He says he prefers to read other types of books. He includes some of the same plot points as Yoshe, and also puts the book and author information at the beginning of his review. Kavi and Yoshe have different viewpoints on the book, but neither of them is incorrect. Reviews and other argumentative writing are based on one's personal opinion.

Movie reviews follow pretty much the same format as book reviews. You will likely have different things to include. Special effects may be a factor in your enjoyment of the movie. You may appreciate a character, but think the actor was not very good in the part. Many movies are also based on books, so a movie review can also include a book review. Let's look at a movie review written by Jamar for school.

Last week I saw a movie called <u>My Friend Totoro</u>, which is animated and about these kids in Japan who befriend Totoro, a creature who is the spirit of the forest. Totoro starts out seeming big and scary, but then the kids realize he's nice, and he protects the trees and makes things grow. There are magical elements in the movie. The kids in the story are sisters, and at one point there's a crisis involving one of them that leads to lots of action and some adventure. The movie truly has great animation. It's not too scary, so even small kids can see it. I really liked it and would see it again. I recommend it highly.

Jamar does a good job of explaining why he likes the movie. Now let's see what Martine thought of it.

The movie <u>My Friend Totoro</u> was at the Bijou last week, and I went to see it with my dad. It's an animated movie by a Japanese moviemaker. I'm not a big fan of animation, and never really liked cartoons, but my dad said it was supposed to be good, so we went. I was surprised by how much I enjoyed it. The animation was different from the cartoons I never really liked. It was a cartoon, but also looked real in some ways. The story was completely fantastic and unbelievable, which I guess is to be expected in animation. Since I'm really a nonfiction person, I couldn't really get into the part of the story about Totoro being the forest spirit. I think other kids would like the movie, though, especially if they like animation.

Martine did not like the movie as much as Jamar did, but explains why, and still recommends the film to others. As with the book reviews discussed earlier, two people can have very different reactions to a book or movie. It's only important that you express your response clearly and concisely.

Example 1

The book *The Hobbit* by J.R.R. Tolkien is the prequel to the *Lord of the Rings* series by this author. It follows the adventures of a hobbit named Bilbo Baggins, who would rather stay at home in his warm hobbit hole. But he is chosen by the wizard Gandalf to go with a group of dwarves on a search for treasure. He has scary, magical, and exciting experiences along the way, and in the end he returns home to live out his days quietly. It's a well-written and really fun book, and I recommend it to anyone who likes science fiction and adventure stories.

1 **What is the viewpoint of the author of this review?**

A The book is well written and a great read.

B The book is for fans of the *Lord of the Rings* trilogy.

C Hobbits are strange creatures.

D The book is fun but not a great story.

Coach What information should a review provide right up front for the reader?

Example 2

The Muppet Christmas Carol is another version of the Charles Dickens' story "A Christmas Carol." This movie has a cartoon effect because of the Muppets, but it also has human cast members, including Michael Caine. Kermit the Frog is Bob Cratchett, and Miss Piggy is his wife. Gonzo and Rizzo the Rat are very funny. It's too scary for very small kids.

2   **Is this a well-written review? What might make it better?**

_____

_____

_____

_____

_____

SELF
Coach   Discuss your answer with your teacher or class.

Coached Reading

This editorial is about a town meeting. As you read the editorial, use the statements and questions in the margin to help your understanding.

 Your teacher may read this selection to you.

1. Last Thursday there was a town meeting on the Community College campus. Did you know there was one? I sure didn't.

The people who set up the meetings never let people know about them. I work long days and can't always come to meetings in the afternoon. Lots of people have that problem. Or they work nights and can't make it to the meetings. I wanted to go to the meeting last week to protest the increase in tolls on the expressway to pay for the new subway stop. I can't take the subway and shouldn't have to pay for other people to do so. I would have liked to tell them that at the meeting. They should have the meetings at a more convenient location, for people who live downtown. They could have more than one meeting on each topic. Now they'll take action on the toll increase without hearing from people who don't want it. I couldn't make it to the meeting.

Can you tell what the author's viewpoint is?

Does the author provide reasons why the reader should agree with his position?

This editorial about a local election campaign. As you read the editorial, use the statements and questions in the margin to help your understanding.

 Your teacher may read this selection to you.

2. The candidates in the local town council election owe it to the voters to stop their negative campaigning. When candidates spend all their time and energy telling voters how awful the other candidates are, no one is well served. The candidates all look petty, and the voters have no idea what the candidates really stand for.

What is this author's position?

I have very little faith in any of the candidates. If they want my vote, they need to stand up, separate themselves from the negative campaigning, and give me a reason to vote for them. Many other citizens feel the way I do including my mailman. We are tired of always hearing one candidate say bad things about another. Where do you stand on the school district budget? Do you plan to approve the sales tax increase? Will you support the prescription drug plan? These are the issues that truly matter to voters, and if we don't find a candidate who can offer us real answers, we won't come out on election day.

Is this editorial concise and effective? Is there nonessential information that should be deleted?

Re-read the editorials, and ask yourself the questions in the margin again. Then answer questions 1 through 3.

1 The author's position in editorial 2 is that

A elections are a waste of time

B candidates should stop negative campaigning

C everyone has the right to vote

D she's not voting this year

2 Is editorial 1 well constructed and concisely written? Why or why not?

_____

_____

_____

_____

_____

3 In what ways are the editorials alike?

F They both suggest that voting is unfair.

G They are both well-written arguments.

H They both want people to come out and vote.

J They both include unnecessary details.

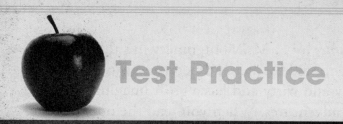

Test Practice

Read the these reviews of *Anne of Green Gables*. Then answer questions 1 through 3.

1. The book *Anne of Green Gables* by L. M. Montgomery was required reading for my English class this year. The book tells the story of Anne Shirley, an orphan who comes to live at Green Gables, a farm on Prince Edward Island in Canada. She is adopted by Matthew and Merilla Cuthbert, a middle-aged brother and sister who wanted to adopt a boy to help out on the farm. Anne arrives by train instead, and the Cuthberts don't have the heart to send her back to the orphanage.

So Anne is adopted and settles into life at the farm. She has a wonderful imagination and forms a fast friendship with her neighbor, Diana. Anne is very independent, and she gets caught up in lots of adventures, large and small: she bakes a cake with a spearmint liniment in place of vanilla; she tries to dye her red hair black and turns it green; she takes a dare to walk along the edge of a roof and falls and breaks her ankle. Anne grows up in the book, and comes to love her life in Green Gables, where there is, as she says, plenty of "scope of imagination."

Matthew loves Anne immediately, but it takes Merilla longer to warm up to her. Merilla takes the responsibility for raising Anne very seriously, and is very no-nonsense. She doesn't understand Anne's imaginative ways, but she comes to love her. The book is interesting and funny, and the reader will grow to love Anne just as Merilla does. Elementary and middle school readers will really enjoy this book.

2. Recently I read *Anne of Green Gables* by L. M. Montgomery. It's the story of an orphan named Anne Shirley who is adopted by the Cuthberts and moves to a farm called Green Gables. Anne is funny and witty and has a great imagination. She carries the reader along with her on her adventures. When you read the book, you feel like you know Anne, and she's one of your own friends.

She wants certain clothes, and she complains about her red hair. She has a temper and isn't used to having a family. I usually like to read science fiction books, and I really like author Ursula K. Le Guin. There's no science fiction in this book. If science fiction is your favorite, you might not like this book, but it's pretty interesting anyway.

1 The author's viewpoint in review 1 is that

A   *Anne of Green Gables* is a great book

B   most people will find *Anne of Green Gables* too silly

C   Anne Shirley had trouble adjusting to life at Green Gables

D   reading books is good for you

2   The author of review 2 believes

F   L.M. Montgomery is a better writer than Ursula K. LeGuin

G   Anne Shirley is a convincing heroine

H   *Anne of Green Gables* is not for everyone

J   *Anne of Green Gables* should be required reading in English classes

3   Which of the two reviews presents a stronger, more convincing argument? Explain your answer on the lines below, using examples from the reviews to support your answer.

_____

_____

_____

_____

_____

_____

_____

_____

_____

_____

_____

_____

NOTICE: Photocopying any part of this book is forbidden by law.

175

Performance Indicators: W.3.b, W.3.c, W.3.e, W.3.f

CHAPTER 7

Writing Nonfiction and Persuasive Texts

Lesson 23: Writing Argument

When writing a persuasive essay, your first goal is to state your position clearly. Your point of view on the subject of your essay is the most important part of your essay. Identify the issue you are going to write about and explain your position at the beginning of your paper. *Always* begin your essay or editorial by stating your position. This will make it clear to the reader what the writing is about and what argument you are trying to make.

If you were writing a letter to the school newspaper about an upcoming election and you wanted your fellow students to vote for the candidate you were supporting, it might look something like this:

> Later this month, the students of P.S. 80 will elect a new president of the student body. We will be choosing between Jessie Alvarez and Samir Gupta. I ask all of you to vote for Jessie. She has the highest grade average in the school, so she has proven herself to be smart and dedicated. Jessie also belongs to the chess club and led her teammates to a citywide championship. She has some great ideas for improving this school, but it won't happen unless we elect her. Let's all make the right decision. Vote for Jessie!

Try to structure your argument with positive supporting information: present your argument as being *in favor of* something, rather than *against* something. Review the sample on page 176 again. You will notice that the writer could have argued <u>against</u> Samir; but instead, the writer argued <u>for</u> Jessie. Trying to persuade someone to do something is often easier and more effective than trying to persuade someone to stop doing something. Here is the same passage, but this time it is written with a negative argument:

> Later this month, the students of P.S. 80 will elect a new president of the student body. We will be choosing either Jessie Alvarez or Samir Gupta. I ask you all to vote for Jessie. Samir would make a terrible student body president. His grades are average at best, and he has never joined a club or team. He doesn't seem to care about the school or the students. He will not improve things in the school in any way. Voting for Samir would be the worst decision ever.

When you take a position in support of something in your writing, you use positive, supportive language, so the reader is more likely to come away with a positive image of what you have to say. When you speak out against something, on the other hand, you use negative language, which leaves the reader thinking negative thoughts.

Supporting Your Position

After you have stated your position, you need to support it in order to persuade others to feel the same way. The two most effective tools for doing this are

- relevant evidence
- effective emotional appeals

Relevant evidence includes any information that relates to the issue and supports the position you are making. It is the details that prove your thesis statement. For example, if you were arguing in favor of recycling in your community, relevant evidence would include information about how much money other cities and towns have saved over time by starting a recycling program, how a great number of the people in your community support a recycling program, and how much cleaner the community would be if people recycled.

NOTICE: Photocopying any part of this book is forbidden by law.

177

If the evidence is not relevant, it will not help your case very much. In fact, introducing evidence that is not relevant could backfire if the reader thinks that the writer lacks knowledge and understanding of the issue. When gathering evidence to support your position, stay focused on the purpose of your composition.

People do not make decisions based entirely on what they *think*. They often decide to do or not to do something based at least in part on the way they *feel*. For this reason, you should also include effective emotional appeals when appropriate. In your argument for a recycling program, you might include an emotional appeal that reminds the reader of a simpler time, when people cared about their community and worked hard to keep it clean. You could also include an appeal to live up to parents' and grandparents' values and hopes and dreams for the community. You could also express a wish for a future in which your children have a cleaner, safer place to live, and where they have grown up with strong beliefs and a work ethic that does not allow wasting resources that can be reused.

When you make an emotional appeal, you address the reader's heart, not just his mind. When you are trying to convince someone to agree with your position, including the right emotional appeal could be what is necessary to help you succeed.

Organizing Your Argument

When you have decided what your position is and the methods you'll use to support your position, your next step is deciding how to organize your argument.

- Make sure to grab your reader's attention in the introduction.
- Organize your points in order of importance.
- Save your strongest point for last.
- If you're having trouble deciding which points are strongest, think about which one you have the most to say about. That could be your strongest point.

Addressing Your Reader's Concerns

When writing a persuasive essay, it is important to remember that your argument has to include your reader's concerns. In other words, you should respond to the major points readers might make against your argument.

- Think about the issue you will be writing about and then identify how that issue will most likely affect your readers.
- Keep in mind that your reader may hold a different point of view. This means that you will have to find a way to change his or her mind

Identifying Your Audience

In order to address your reader's concerns, you first need to identify your reader, and then adjust your writing to make it appropriate for that reader.

When you are writing about a very technical subject, for example, you would not need to explain technical terms if your reader were an expert in that field.

Sometimes you know who your audience is. When you write an essay for class, for example, the reader is usually your teacher or your classmates. When you know who your audience is, you can adjust your writing style and tone to a manner that is appropriate for the audience. For example, the way you write for your teacher will likely differ from the way you write for your classmates. You would probably be more formal with your teacher than with your classmates. This is diction, which we discussed in Lesson 3.

Unfortunately, you do not always know exactly who your audience is. Sometimes you have to make an educated guess. For example, let's say that you are writing that editorial for the local newspaper. Your audience would be anybody who reads the newspaper. Who is most likely to read the newspaper?

First, your newspaper reader is probably an adult. Far more adults than children read newspapers. Second, the person is probably someone who is interested in what is going on in the world. Third, you are writing an editorial. What kind of person reads this section of the paper? Someone interested in local opinions and views. Based on these factors, your reader is an adult living in your town who is interested in the local opinions and views. While this is still a pretty general idea of the person you are writing for, you have at least determined *some* of his or her concerns.

Example 1

1 **You are writing an editorial in favor of cutting school taxes paid by the elderly. Which of the following would NOT be considered relevant evidence?**

A The elderly have paid a great deal of money over time in school taxes because they have lived in this community longer than younger families have, so they deserve a break.

B More children need to be able to attend college when they graduate from high school.

C The extra tax money collected last year could be used to make up for the tax cut for the elderly.

D The elderly do not have children in school, so they should not have to contribute as much to the local school district as families with school-age children.

Which choice would be the least important to include?

NOTICE: Photocopying any part of this book is forbidden by law.

181

Example 2

2 **Which of the following would be an effective emotional appeal to persuade people to support a school tax cut for the elderly?**

F   By reducing costs, we can afford to cut school taxes for everyone.

G   If we cut taxes now, schools will have to buy fewer supplies and cut school programs.

H   How can we ask these people, our own parents and grandparents, to sacrifice even more, after they've given us so much throughout our lives?

J   The time is not right for a school tax cut for anyone for any reason.

 Which choice appeals to the heart more than to the brain?

Example 3

3 Now, it's time for you to begin writing your own editorial. You will complete this editorial at the end of this chapter. Using your own paper, write

a) an outline for an editorial to be published in your school paper on the topic below

b) only the <u>introduction</u> to your editorial

Be sure to

- identify why you are writing the editorial and the position you are taking
- provide relevant evidence and/or emotional appeals to support your position
- organize your argument, saving your strongest points for last
- address the concerns of your reader

Editorial Topic: Lunch in the Cafeteria

Your school's cafeteria has always served the same thing for lunch: peanut butter and jelly sandwiches. They are good, but you are tired of having the same lunch every day. You want the school board to step in and require the cafeteria to change the menu. Suggest some other types of food they could serve, and explain why it would be smart for them to do so.

Performance Indicators: R.1.k, W.1.a, W.1.d, W.3.b

Lesson 24
Writing Research Reports

The purpose of a research report is to discover and present information on a topic. The information you include in your research report may come from many different sources, such as books, magazines, newspapers, journals, or experts you interview. Finding the information you need for your paper is called performing research.

Once you have completed your research, you must organize everything you've learned about your topic and write a paper that tells others about what you discovered. In this lesson, you'll practice some of the skills you need to write a research report.

Before you can begin researching, you need a topic. Unless your teacher gives you a specific topic to write about, you should always choose a topic that interests you. It's also helpful if your topic is one that has been of interest to others, because there will be material written on the topic that you can use to research your report.

Here are some topics for a research paper. Choose one of these for the exercises on the next page. You may also think of one on your own.

- Who were the Wright Brothers?
- Why is New York a great city?
- Who invented the food pyramid?
- What is a star?

- What is the importance of Ellis Island?
- How does television work?
- How does a hot air balloon work?

Example 1

1   **Now that you've chosen a topic, it's time to brainstorm ideas about it. For a reminder on how to brainstorm, review Lesson 15. Use the following lines to brainstorm your research topic.**

My topic is: _____

_____

_____

_____

_____

_____

_____

_____

_____

_____

Example 2

2   **Review your brainstormed list. What ideas stand out the most? What ideas interest you? Now, freewrite for two minutes on your topic. For a reminder on how to freewrite, review Lesson 15. Use your own paper to brainstorm your research topic.**

Example 3

3 Review the brainstorming and freewriting exercises you completed on your research topic. You may now have enough information to begin a loose outline for your research paper. Create your outline in the space below. On the lines with the Roman numerals, write your two topic sentences. Write details supporting those sentences on the other lines. Remember, if you decide to write a research paper on this topic, you'll need to go to the library and do some research. The purpose of this outline is to give you a place to begin.

I. _____

    A. _____

    B. _____

    C. _____

II. _____

    A. _____

    B. _____

    C. _____

Lesson 25: Summarizing, Quoting, and Paraphrasing

Sometimes when you write nonfiction, you need to give readers information you've found in another place. For example, you may be writing a book report and want to tell your readers about the book. Maybe you've seen a movie and want to write a review about it for the school newspaper. How do you give readers just enough information without telling them everything?

You can use several strategies:

- summarizing
- quoting
- paraphrasing

We'll discuss each of these in this lesson.

A **summary** is a brief description of a text in your own words. The writer of the summary retells the most important details from the original text to give the reader a good idea of what the original was about. A summary includes information about the main idea and the supporting details. It does not include *all* of the details from the text.

A book report is a good example of a summary. The writer tells the reader what the most important points in the book were.

A summary of *Pete's a Pizza* by William Steig would look something like this—

> A boy named Pete wants to go out and play ball with his friends, but it's raining outside. He sits inside, sulking, and in a bad mood. Pete's dad decides to make him into a pizza, and he puts Pete on the table, and puts pretend toppings on him. He then puts him in a pretend oven to cook, and then puts him back on the table to eat him. Pete gets up and runs away. When he nears the door, he sees that it has stopped raining, and he goes outside to play.

When creating your summary, you can look back at the text you are summarizing, but use your own words in the summary. Your summary could be a page, a paragraph, or a sentence, depending on the length of the material you are summarizing and the space you have for your summary. The hard part about writing a summary is knowing what to put in and what to leave out.

Here's another summary of *Pete's a Pizza*, this time in a couple of sentences:

> A boy who is sad because it's raining and he can't play outside is cheered up by his dad. Before he knows it, the rain has stopped and he can go outside.

Look at the original summary to see which details the 2-sentence version leaves out.

Another useful way to present information from a passage is by quoting what another person or source has said or written. **Quotations**, or quotes for short, are the exact words a person or source uses. They appear between quotation marks. Use quotes when the exact words are necessary or very interesting. For example, a quotation can be useful if you find that a source has said something in a very useful or colorful way, and you lose the effect of that when you try to put it in your own words. You would also use quotations to present the exact words of someone you interviewed in your research.

Here are some examples of the correct use of quotations:

- William Shakespeare wrote, "That which we call a rose by any other name would smell as sweet."
- Movie critic Sue Chen described the actress as "the perfect blend of raw talent and natural grace."

Notice that in every example, the source of the quotation—who said or wrote it—appears along with the quotation itself. Your reader should have no doubt who said or wrote anything you are quoting. This is called citing a source.

A final strategy you can use to include information from another source in your own writing is to **paraphrase** it. Like a summary, you use your own words to describe what happened in a text. A paraphrase is different from a summary in that a paraphrase will restate more of the text and include more of the details. A paraphrase can be as long as the original, but a summary will be much shorter. You should paraphrase when the exact words aren't necessary or particularly interesting. You can also paraphrase when the original words are difficult or confusing and need to be reworded so that your reader can understand them. When you paraphrase or summarize, you don't need to use quotation marks, because you will be putting the information into your own words.

Read the passage below.

Original

Many people find penguins to be rather funny-looking. However, they are fascinating creatures. Penguins are birds, but because of their heavy skeletons, they are unable to fly. They are fantastic swimmers, though. They use their tail and webbed feet for steering underwater. Penguins are also first-rate hunters. They dive underwater to find fish and other things to eat. They cannot breathe underwater, so they come up to the surface to take short breaths, then dive back in again.

Now read a student's paraphrase of this passage below.

Paraphrase

Some people think that penguins are odd-looking, but these are very interesting animals. Although they are birds, penguins cannot fly because their skeleton weighs too much. Still, they are great swimmers. Their webbed feet and tail help them make their way underwater and find fish and other food. They are excellent hunters. Because they are unable to breathe underwater, penguins have to rise to the surface to breathe. Then they dive into the water again.

You can see that the paraphrase contains the same details of the original in the same order, but the paraphrase is in the student's own words.

When you paraphrase, cite the source like you would when you quote. A paraphrase is not put in quotation marks because you are putting the information into your own words. However, you should still give credit to your source. And this holds true whether you are paraphrasing a sentence or a paragraph or more. Below are some examples of how you can give credit to a source when you paraphrase.

- Sherry McNeil believes that penguins are interesting animals.
- According to Sherry McNeil, penguins are great swimmers.
- Sherry McNeil writes that penguins are too heavy to fly.

These are not the only ways to cite a source. But introducing the paraphrase by referring to the author is a common way. Sometimes you may lead into a paraphrase by citing the title of the work. For example,

- *World Book Encyclopedia* says that the penguins are unable to breathe underwater and must rise to the surface to breathe.

Not every single piece of information that you get from a source will have to be credited. For example, you may have to look in the encyclopedia to learn that Abraham Lincoln was the 16th President. But even though you had to check, this is still considered general, or common, knowledge. You could include this detail in a report without having to cite the encyclopedia. If you are ever not sure when to cite, check with your teacher.

Example 1

The island of Puerto Rico is known for its beautiful beaches, amazing rain forest, and tasty traditional dishes. However, it might be just as famous for a very small creature that lives there. The coquí is a frog that is found in great numbers throughout the island. Coquís can be as small as a half-inch in length. They get their name from their song. They come out at night and sing "coquí, coquí" until the sun comes up. Even when people depart from the island, the song of the coquí is a sound they never forget.

1a   **Now write a paraphrase of this passage on the lines below.**

Remember to use as much of your own words as possible.

Performance Indicator: W.CPI.7

Lesson 26
Writing a Bibliography

When researching and writing, it is important that you record the sources you use for information. When you take notes, write down the information on each source you use before you begin taking notes. You need to record this information carefully and correctly so that you give proper credit to your sources. This also allows your readers to find the information you used if they wish.

You will use the information you recorded on each source to create a bibliography. A **bibliography** is a list of resources used in researching a paper. The bibliography lists all of the books, magazines, and other sources the writer used. A bibliography uses standardized formats that must always be followed. Bibliographic references are organized alphabetically, by the first letter in the first word of each citation.

How do you know what information you will need to record for each source? On the next page are examples of how to list different sources in a bibliography. Use these to create a bibliography, and also to find out what information you need to record for each source in the bibliography. There are many different formats for creating a bibliography; just remember these two important things:

1. When in doubt about how to write an entry, include as much information as you can, so that your readers will be certain where to find your source.
2. Be consistent: make sure, for example, that all the book listings match.

Let's look at some sample bibiographic entries on the next page.

Book with One Author

Author's last name, Author's first name. *Book title*. City of publication: Publisher, Publication date.

Example: Barnes, Phillip. *Undersea Exploration*. Chicago: Indigo Press, 1984.

Book with Multiple Authors

Author names should be given in the same order they are given in the book.

First author's last name, First author's first name, and Second author's last name, Second author's first name. *Book title*. City of publication: Publisher, Publication date.

Example: Durocher, Otto, and Belize, Alice. *Aeronautical Engineering*. Los Angeles: Spike Publications, 1976.

Encyclopedia

If the author's name is not available, use the editor's name. If neither is available, begin with the title of the article.

Author's last name, Author's first name. "Article Title." *Publication Title*. Edition. Publication year.

Example: Jones, Belle. "Agriculture." *Harper Encyclopedia of Science*. 15th ed. 2001.

Periodical Article (Magazine or Newspaper)

Author's last name, Author's first name. "Article Title." *Periodical Title* date month year: page.

Example: Stanford, Greg. "New Museum Opens." *Montreal News* 18 Aug. 1995: A14.

Online Article

Make sure with Internet sources that you list the date you found the information. The final piece of an Internet bibliographic entry should be the Web address, so that your reader can find it again. Online articles often do not have an author. If this is the case, begin the listing with the article title. Some online articles will actually tell you at the bottom of the page how you should cite them in your bibliography.

Author's last name, Author's first name. "Article Title." Website name. Online. Internet Day month year of access. Available Web site address.

Example: "The First Thanksgiving." Scholastic website. Online. Internet 16 January 2005. Available http://teacher.scholastic.com/thanksgiving/

Example 1

1 **Which of the following is the correct format for a bibliography entry for a newspaper article?**

A Bill Cunningham. "Autumn Mix." *The New York Times* 31 October 2004: ST4(L).

B Cunningham, Bill. "Autumn Mix." *The New York Times* 31 October 2004: ST4(L).

C Cunningham, Bill. *Autumn Mix*. The New York Times October 31, 2004, ST4(L).

D Cunningham, Bill, "Autumn Mix." *The New York Times* October 31, 2004: ST4(L).

Look back at the formats to see which entry is correctly formatted.

Example 2

2 **Which of the following is the correct bibliographic entry for a book called Stars, written by Ann Lee and published by Dale Press of Austin in 2002?**

F Ann Lee. "Stars" Austin: Dale Press, 2002.

G Lee, Ann. "Stars." Austin: Dale Press, 2002.

H Lee, Ann. Stars. Austin: Dale Press: 2002.

J Lee, Ann. *Stars*. Austin: Dale Press, 2002.

Discuss your answer with your teacher or class.

Writing Practice

Now you are ready to draft the editorial you began in Lesson 23. Look back at the outline you created and at your introduction, and review the topic provided in the lesson. The topic is repeated below.

Your school's cafeteria has always served the same thing for lunch: peanut butter and jelly sandwiches. They are good, but you are tired of having the same lunch every day. You want the school board to step in and require the cafeteria to change the menu. Suggest some other types of food they could serve, and explain why it would be smart for them to do so.

Do your outline and introduction address the topic? Have you presented your topic and your position clearly in your introduction? Now is your chance to make changes to the outline and introduction. When you are ready, on your own paper, draft your editorial.

Remember to

- identify why you are writing the editorial and the position you are taking at the beginning of your editorial
- provide relevant evidence and/or emotional appeals to support your position
- organize your argument, saving your strongest point for last
- address the concerns of your reader

Use the Editing Checklist on the next page to edit your editorial after you are finished.

Editing Checklist

1 Check your capitalization and punctuation.

2 Spell all words correctly.

3 Check for sentence fragments or run-on sentences.

4 Keep verb tense consistent.

5 Make sure subjects and verbs agree.

6 Use words according to the rules of Standard English.

7 Remember to paragraph correctly.

UNIT

II Reading and Writing about Literature

GETTING THE IDEA

In this unit, you'll review some skills that you need to read and write about literature. In the following four chapters, this Unit will help you:

- identify the features of different types of fiction texts
- read and analyze fiction texts
- identify different forms of poetry
- understand key elements of fiction, including plot, character, setting, and theme
- understand the meaning of dialogue and stage directions in drama
- identify and understand metephor, simile, symbolism, personification, and foreshadowing
- write your own poems
- write more effective responses to short-response questions

By the end of this unit, you will be a better reader and writer of fiction.

Performance Indicators: R.2.a, R.2.b, R.2.e, R.2.g, L.2.a, L.2.c

CHAPTER 8

Types of Literature

Lesson 27: Poetry

Poetry is a very expressive form of writing that uses rhythm and rhyme to convey emotion. Poems are usually easy to recognize because of their structure. A poem generally takes the form of a series of short lines of text, each of which may or may not be a complete sentence. Other identifying characteristics of poetry include the following:

- **stanzas**—groups of lines into which a poem is divided
- **rhythm**—a structured pattern of sounds, alternating between weak and strong or sound and silence, creating a regular beat
- **rhyme**—when words end with the same sound
- **imagery**—words that make pictures in your mind

Poems are often shorter than other types of literature. Because of its use of stanzas, poetry looks different from fiction or drama. Like prose, however, poetry can tell a story. Though you may not realize it, you often hear poetry in everyday life. The songs you hear on the radio and in commercials are often simply poems set to music. Remember Mother Goose? Nursery rhymes are also poetry.

Read the passage below, then answer the question that follows.

Excerpt from "Trees," by Joyce Kilmer

I think that I shall never see
A poem lovely as a tree

Name two rhyming words from this poem.

_____

_____

_____

 Look at the ends of the lines. Do the end-of-line words sound alike?

As noted earlier, poetry has some essential features: it's broken into lines and stanzas, and it uses rhythm and sometimes rhyme.

Words that rhyme sound alike. Grow," "know," and "show" rhyme—they sound the same. Not all poetry uses rhyme, but when a poem uses a rhyming structure, its lines end with rhyming words. A rhyming poem usually uses rhyme in a pattern: rhyming words may appear at the end of every line or at the end of every other line. Two consecutive lines of verse that rhyme are called a **couplet**. The lines in a couplet work together in a poem to create a unit, though the unit may not be a sentence.

Note the end-of-line rhyme of "see" and "tree" in the couplet above. A great way to figure out whether a poem rhymes is to read it out loud, and listen for the words that sound alike.

Rhyme and Meter

Not all poetry uses rhyme, but it will use rhythm. **Rhythm** is the sound of the lines of poetry when they are read, or how the voice of the reader rises and falls when reading a poem aloud. This is the sound of stressed and unstressed syllables in words. Using the stresses in words, poets create rhythmic patterns called **meter**. You can discover the meter of a poem by figuring out which syllables are stressed in each line. To do this, count the number of sounds (or beats) in each line, not the number of words. Then figure out which words are stressed. Look at two lines from the nursery rhyme:

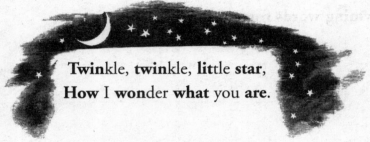

Twinkle, **twin**kle, **lit**tle **star**,
How I **won**der **what** you **are**.

In each line, the words or parts of words that are stressed appear in bold. The first line has four words and seven syllables, or beats. Four of those syllables are stressed—they are emphasized when the words are spoken. The pattern of stressed and unstressed beats gives a poem its meter.

Like rhyme, meter can more easily be *heard* than *read*. In the lines from the nursery rhyme above, you can easily hear the rhyme and meter when you say the lines aloud.

Poems often use expressive language, such as imagery. **Imagery** can be described as the words in poetry or fiction that appeal to one or more of the senses: sight, taste, touch, hearing, and smell. Describing clouds as "billowing," for example, or the "bitter, pulpy taste of a lemon" are examples of imagery. They help the reader imagine more clearly what the writer is trying to express.

Types of Poems

There are many different types of poems, each with its own features. Let's take a look at some of the most common forms of poetry.

Ballad

A ballad is a very old form of song that tells a story, often about something sad or tragic. A ballad usually rhymes. Most folk songs are ballads. Some examples of ballads you may be familiar with are "Darling Clementine," "Oh Susanna," and "Old Dan Tucker."

Excerpt from traditional ballad "Barbara Allen"

'Twas in the merry month of May
When green buds all were swelling
Sweet William on his death-bed lay
For the love of Barbara Allen

He sent his servant to the town
To the place where she was dwelling
Saying, You must come to my master dear
If your name be Barbara Allen.

Lyric

When you hear the word *lyric*, you may think of the words to a song. But a lyric is also a type of poetry—poetry that was originally written to be sung. The word *lyric* comes from lyre, a harplike instrument played by ancient Greek poets during poetry recitals. A lyric is pretty much any short poem. The sonnet, the elegy, and the ode are types of lyric poems.

Excerpt from "Bed in Summer," by Robert Louis Stevenson

In winter I get up at night
And dress by yellow candle-light.
In summer, quite the other way,
I have to go to bed by day.
I have to go to bed and see
The birds still hopping on the tree,
Or hear the grown-up people's feet
Still going past me in the street.

Ode

An ode is a type of lyric poem that praises something or someone. The word *ode* comes from the Greek *oide*, meaning "song." An ode may be written for a particular occasion, or be a poem recognizing an important person, place, or thing.

Excerpt from "Summer Day" by Horace Elgin

The glory of a summer day,
With sunshine bright and field and hedge,
A shimmering blacktop leads the way,
Meandering to water's edge.
The ocean calls to me, I hear
Her voice so strong and sweet
I heed her call and soon am near—
I feel the sand beneath my feet.

Sonnet

A sonnet is a rhymed lyric poem of 14 lines. While the subject matter of a sonnet can vary wildly, the form—14 lines—is a rule for the style.

"The Terrier" by Luisa Armenas

My best friend is a terrier,
She could be no hairier—
Full of fun, small but strong,
She strains the leash as we walk along
The sidewalk near my home.
Look, gleaming in our path—a bone!
With a terrific growl she pounces,
Like a wolf that weighs just 16 ounces.
Ferociously, she starts to gnaw,
Guarding her find with tiny paws.
This would be a funny sight
Were it not the middle of the night.
If I don't drag her home, to bed—
She'll spend all night right here, instead.

Limerick

A limerick is a silly or humorous poem that rhymes. Limericks have five lines: lines 1, 2 and 5 rhyme, and lines 3 and 4 also rhyme. The topic of a limerick is usually silly.

A limerick by Edward Lear

There was a Young Lady whose eyes,
Were unique as to colour and size;
When she opened them wide,
People all turned aside,
And started away in surprise.

Haiku

Haiku is a traditional form of Japanese poetry. Haiku is one type of poem that doesn't rhyme, but it does have very specific requirements for form: a haiku has three lines and 17 syllables. The syllables are broken across the lines as follows:

- Line 1 has 5 syllables
- Line 2 has 7 syllables
- Line 3 has 5 syllables

Because the haiku is very short, it can be fun to practice. It can be difficult to stick with the syllable requirement, though.

Haiku by Matsuo Basho

Ah! The ancient pond
As the green frog takes the plunge
Sound of the water.

Example 1

To a Houseplant

by Harry Mendez

Last week you were in your prime,
a dark green mass of leaf and vine.
Your tendrils wound around the curtains
and up the walls, and I made certain
to follow advice from each book I read—
I kept you watered, kept you fed,
gave you only indirect light,
played classical music for you each night.
But soon your leaves yellowed and spotted,
your stems turned brown and all your roots rotted.
No matter what I do to help them thrive,
I just can't keep houseplants alive.

1 **This poem is an example of a**

A limerick

B ode

C haiku

D couplet

What is the content of the poem? How about the structure? What form of poetry is it most like?

Example 2

By Issa

Giant firefly:
that way, this way, that way, this—
and it passes by

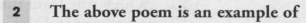

2 **The above poem is an example of**

F a ballad

G a limerick

H a haiku

J a sonnet

Read the poem out loud. What do you notice? Does it rhyme? What is its format?

Example 3

From The Walrus and the Carpenter

by Lewis Carroll

The sun was shining on the sea,
    Shining with all his might:
He did his very best to make
    The billows smooth and bright—
And this was odd, because it was
    The middle of the night.

The moon was shining sulkily,
    Because she thought the sun
Had got no business to be there
    After the day was done—
'It's very rude of him,' she said,
    'To come and spoil the fun!'

3 **Which line from the poem shows something imaginary and not something real?**

  A "The sun was shining on the sea"

  B "The middle of the night"

  C "After the day was done"

  D "The moon was shining sulkily"

SELF
Coach

Discuss your answer with your teacher or class.

Lesson 28
Fiction

Fiction is any type of story that describes imaginary people or events, or that tells a tale that is not factual. Any type of story that came from the mind of the writer is considered fiction. Examples of fiction include novels and short stories. Nonfiction texts contain factual information, and fiction texts are made-up stories.

Some types of fiction began long ago, and were handed down orally, or by word of mouth—this was before there were printed books. Other types are more recent additions to the world of literature. Some common types of fiction are described below.

A **myth** is a traditional story featuring heroes or supernatural beings. Myths often explore the origins of things, such as the Earth or the weather. There are many different versions of such myths, which are based on the beliefs of a particular culture. A Native American myth credits the creation of the Earth to the sky woman, who falls into a hole and is saved by a turtle, who becomes the Earth. In Greek mythology, a bird named Nyx lays an egg, and when it hatched, the god of love came out, and the two halves of the eggshell became the sky and the Earth. Myths are often about large or serious themes, such as gods, death and love.

A **legend** is a story that has been passed down for generations. It may be about someone or something real, but the story is unlikely to be completely true. Like myths, legends are basic to a certain culture. There are legends about many historical figures. The legend of Johnny Appleseed, for example, is based on the life of John Chapman. Often, legends exaggerate or invent details to stress certain qualities of the main character. John Chapman, for example, did grow apple trees, but he did not spread them throughout the west, and he did not wear a pot on his head, as the legend says.

Read the passage below, then answer the question that follows.

When he was a boy, George Washington chopped down a cherry tree. When asked about it, he confessed, saying, "Father, I cannot tell a lie." Young George was not punished for his action.

What type of fiction is this?

_____

_____

_____

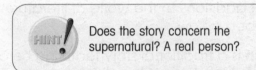 Does the story concern the supernatural? A real person?

Fables are brief stories that teach a lesson or moral, which might be stated at the end of the story. Fables usually feature animal characters. The most famous fables are those of a Greek slave named Aesop, who lived about 600 BC—fables have been around a long time. One of Aesop's best-known fables is "The Tortoise and the Hare," in which the two animals race, and the tortoise wins because the hare is overly confident, and naps during the race. When he awakens and heads toward the goal, he sees that the tortoise has beaten him there. The moral of the fable: *Slow but steady wins the race.* Like most fables, the moral is broad and can fit other situations.

A **fairy tale** is a made-up story featuring magical elements, such as fairies and enchanted creatures. They often have a moral message. Famous fairy tales include *Cinderella, Beauty and the Beast,* and *Rumpelstiltskin.*

The **short story** is another common form of fiction. It is a story, like those described above. It is not as old as myths, fables, legends, and fairy tales. The short story is a form of fiction shorter than a novel. It narrates a tale and usually has a main idea, or theme, that tells the reader something about the world. Themes in short stories are often observations on life. For example, a theme might be "money can't buy happiness" or "it's better to lose than to never play the game." Short stories include some basic elements, such as plot, setting, and character; we'll be discussing these in more detail in Chapter 9. An example of the short story is Washington Irving's "The Legend of Sleepy Hollow" and "Rip Van Winkle."

A **novel** is a long work of fiction featuring the same elements as a short story, such as plot, setting, character, and theme. Because novels are long, writers can develop themes and characters more than in a short story. Novels you may be familiar with include Robert Louis Stevenson's *Treasure Island* and *Peter Pan* by J. M. Barrie.

Example 1

1 **What type of fiction would MOST LIKELY include a witch and a fairy godmother?**

A fable

B novel

C fairy tale

D myth

What elements does this story have?
Look back at the types of fiction for clues.

NOTICE: Photocopying any part of this book is forbidden by law.

209

Example 2

The squirrel awoke to pangs of hunger. The morning was bright with August sunlight, and she wanted to find something to eat—quickly. She ran down the tree, and, poised at the edge of the yard, she noticed the garden. She had eaten some delightful strawberries there months ago, but those were gone now. She crept closer to see what remained. Melons: those were difficult to get into, and she could never carry one back to her tree. But look—corn, sweet juicy corn, ready to pick. She scurried through the garden until she could see the plump ears atop high green stalks. She jumped and tried to climb a stalk, but hit something, caught her foot, and, shaking herself free, tumbled back to the ground. There was netting all over the corn! She hadn't seen it at first, but there it was. She tried to dig under the netting, but became entangled in it again. She freed herself, and attempted a few more jumps. Now she was sweating under the mid-morning sun. Weren't there some raspberries at the back fence? She scampered from the garden, glancing back toward the corn. *It's probably hard and dried out, anyway*, she thought.

2a **This passage is an example of which type of fiction?**

A fable

B novel

C fairy tale

D myth

Are there animal characters? Is there a lesson?

2b **The lesson in this story is**

F don't go into the garden in the hot sun

G it's easy to reject something when you can't get it anyway

H look for the netting before you pick your corn

J raspberries are better than corn

Discuss your answer with your teacher or class.

Lesson 29
Drama

We've looked at poetry and fiction, and now it's time to learn about drama. Drama is a little different from both poetry and fiction. While it tells a story like fiction and can be very expressive like poetry, it includes things these other forms of literature both lack. **Drama** is a type of writing generally written to be performed by actors. Some types of drama are plays, television shows, and movies. Some identifying characteristics of a drama include dialogue, stage directions, and scenes.

Dialogue is the words spoken by the characters. Dialogue is used in other forms of writing, but it is the main convention of drama. The story of the play is told through the characters' dialogue, and the characters' motivations are also indicated through what they say. In drama, speech is not usually enclosed in quotation marks, but rather the name of the character speaking is set off from the text, and the dialogue follows. Look at an example dialogue below.

ALTHEA   But, Kate, you really wanted to see that movie.

KATE   I know, Althea, but I can't go on Friday. I have a track meet.

Plays also include **stage directions**, which are instructions for the actors and descriptions of the stage and scenery. When the play is being performed, the audience will not see the stage directions, but will know what is happening from the actions of the characters and changes in scenery. When you are reading a play, the stage directions help you understand where the characters are and what they are doing. These are often italicized to set them apart from the dialogue. They may also be in brackets.

ALTHEA   But, Kate, you really wanted to see that movie.

KATE   I know, Althea, but I can't go on Friday. I have a track meet.

Althea sighs and sits down heavily next to Kate.

Rather than stanzas or chapters, plays are usually divided into acts, and each act may be made up of a number of scenes, or smaller sections of action. Stage directions generally appear with each change of scene to indicate the setting of the play for that scene.

Act One, Scene 4
Deck of a pirate ship at sunset.

 Read the passage below, then answer the question that follows.

Interior, kitchen, evening. Jeffrey and Meg stand at sink, washing dishes.

Meg   I think the party went pretty well.

Jeffrey   They loved the food, that's for sure.

What is the setting of this scene?

_____

_____

 The stage directions include the setting.

Two major types of plays are comedies and tragedies. A **comedy** is a light-hearted drama, written to entertain the audience and make them laugh. Comedies do not often deal with serious subject matter, and have a happy ending. The characters in a comedy will often experience misunderstandings or mishaps that have amusing results. A character might also find himself in an unexpected situation, which also might result in a series of funny incidents. *The Muppet Movie* is an example of a comedy.

Unlike comedy, a **tragedy** deals with serious subject matter and does not have a happy ending. In a tragedy, one of the main characters may have a **tragic flaw** that leads to his or her downfall. The character might be selfish or jealous, and this trait will lead to behavior that causes that person great unhappiness by the end of the play. William Shakespeare's *Romeo and Juliet* is an example of a tragedy.

> **Tragic flaw** Also called *hamartia*. The trait of the hero or heroine of a tragedy that brings about his or her downfall. Common tragic flaws include pride, jealousy, and greed.

Example 1

1 **Which of the following characters would MOST LIKELY be found in a tragedy?**

A twin brothers who pretend to be each other

B a woman who can't stop giggling

C a housepainter who is colorblind

D a king who never listens to good advice

What elements does this story have? Look back at the types of fiction for clues.

NOTICE: Photocopying any part of this book is forbidden by law.

213

Example 2

Scene 2

The scene opens with YOSHE standing on an empty soccer field. She has on workout gear, and has her foot on a soccer ball.

[Enter MARTINE, also in workout gear.]

MARTINE   Hey, Yoshe!

YOSHE   Hi, Martine. I thought you might not be coming.

MARTINE   *[sheepishly]* Yeah, I'm sorry I'm late. I got caught up in the lab. Thanks for doing this, Yoshe.

YOSHE   No problem. I was going to practice anyway.

[Smiling, she kicks the ball to MARTINE, who jumps out of the way, rather than be hit by it.]

YOSHE   *[laughing]* You were supposed to block that, Martine, and then kick it back to me.

MARTINE   *[throwing her hands in the air]* See? I have no idea what I'm doing on a soccer field, Yoshe!

2a **What is the setting for this scene?**

    F   the science lab

    G   the soccer field

    H   inside a school

    J   on the playground

QUICK Coach™   Check the stage directions for the setting.

2b **Is Martine an experienced soccer player? Explain your answer using details from the passage.**

_____

_____

_____

_____

SELF Coach™   Discuss your answer with your teacher or class.

214

Lesson 30
Reading Aloud

In Lesson 20, you learned that it can be helpful to read your own writing aloud to check for errors. In Lesson 27, we recommended that you read poetry aloud because hearing a poem can help you figure out its rhyme and meter. You may sometimes have other reasons: your teacher might ask you to read a poem aloud, or a report, or your class may be reading a play aloud.

Reading in front of others can be nerve-wracking. You want to do a good job, but sometimes you just want it to be over. Well, relax. Breathe. That's your first tip! Here are a few more tips.

Reading Aloud Tips

- Before you read the passage aloud, read it to yourself, noting the tone of the writing and paying attention to the punctuation. A sentence ending in a period should be read differently than one ending in a question mark.

- If you can, read the passage through and make sure you know how to pronounce all of the words. If there are any that you are unsure of, look them up, and practice saying them correctly.

- Once you are familiar with the punctuation and pronunciation, read the passage aloud a few times, practicing the entire passage.

- Speak slowly—try not to rush through, so that you are understood by your audience.

- Speak clearly and loudly enough for others to hear well (but don't yell).

- If you are reading something dramatic, try out your acting skills. If the writing is scary, change your tone of voice and facial expression to show this emotion.

- Try to make eye contact with your audience. Look up from your paper every once in a while. This will help your audience feel more connected to what you are reading.

- Read for an audience—as part of your practice reading, have parents or friends act as your audience. Read your passage to them, and then ask them if you read slowly enough, if they could understand everything you said, and so on. If you're reading a drama, have someone else read the other parts in your practice reading.

- Remember to breathe while you're reading!

Coached Reading

The following passage is about a family getting ready for a trip to the beach. As you read the passage, use the statements and questions in the margin to help your understanding.

 Your teacher may read this selection to you.

Scene 1

Interior, bedroom, night. JACK sits on his bed looking through a magazine. He has on headphones and is dressed casually.

[Enter JACK's MOTHER.]

MOTHER Jack? *[very loudly]* Jack! *[lifts a headphone away from JACK's ear. JACK jumps, startled to see his MOTHER.]*

JACK *[taking off headphones]* Hey, Mom. What's up?

MOTHER Jack, we're leaving tomorrow morning at 5 AM. Are you packed?

JACK Well, no, but it'll only take five minutes. *[smiling]* We're going to the beach. I need flipflops and swim trunks.

MOTHER *[exasperated]* It'll take more than five minutes. You need shorts, sneakers, t-shirts, socks, underwear, something nice for Annie's wedding *[JACK looks down, fiddling with his Discman]*—Jack, are you listening to me?

[JACK looks up, smiles again.]

What is Jack doing in this part of the passage?

How does Jack's mother feel in this section of the passage?

JACK	I hear you, Mom. Something nice for Annie's wedding . . .
MOTHER	And everything else?
JACK	No problem, Mom, except—
MOTHER	Except what?
JACK	*[still smiling]* I think I'm out of underwear. Are you doing laundry before we go?
MOTHER	*[clearly frustrated]* No, I'm not doing laundry! We're leaving at 5 AM, Jack, 5 AM. Get packed, and do your own laundry if you need to. *[Turns and starts to leave.]*
JACK	Oh, Mom?
MOTHER	*[turning]* Yes, Jack?
JACK	I was just kidding. My suitcase is downstairs by the door. Dad said he wanted to load the car tonight.
MOTHER	*[smiling now, too]* Oh, Jack. Get a good night's sleep, okay? *[Kisses him on the head, and leaves the room.]*

[JACK puts headphones back on, and, smiling, picks up his magazine again.]

> If you were reading the part of Jack's mother in this section of the passage, how would you sound? Are you happy? Sad?

> How does Jack's mother change in this part of the passage? Would she sound different than she did earlier?

> **Re-read the passage, and ask yourself the questions in the margin again. Then answer questions 1 through 4.**

1 This passage is set

A at the beach

B in the laundry room

C at school

D in a bedroom

2 The passage can be described as

F a tragedy

G a comedy

H a poem

J a fable

3 In most of the passage, Jack's mother can be described as

A frustrated

B happy

C hungry

D sad

4 Briefly describe what happens in the passage. Use the stage directions for clues.

_____

_____

_____

_____

_____

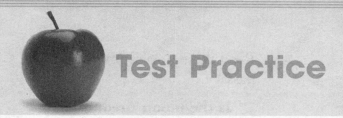

Test Practice

Read this passage about the moon. Then answer questions 1 through 4.

Is the Moon Tired?

by Christina Rossetti

Is the moon tired? She looks so pale
Within her misty veil:
She scales the sky from east to west,
And takes no rest.

Before the coming of the night
The moon shows papery white;
Before the dawning of the day
She fades away.

1 This is an example of

A drama

B fairy tale

C poetry

D novel

2 Which of the following words from the passage rhyme?

F veil, west

G night, white

H night, day

J white, away

3 Read these lines from the passage.

Is the moon tired? She looks so pale/Within her misty veil

These lines are an example of

A sonnet

B dialogue

C stress

D couplet

4 The passage is **mainly** about

F the sunrise

G the rising and setting moon

H being tired at night

J why the moon looks white

Read this passage about John Henry. Then answer questions 5 and 6.

It was 1887, and John Henry was working on a railroad crew. He worked with hundreds of other steel drivers who were working their way through Coosa Mountain in Alabama one swing at a time with their hammers and spikes. Eventually, they'd have a tunnel that the railroad could go through. John Henry was a big, strong man, who stood 6 feet tall and weighed 200 pounds. He could hammer longer and dig more rock than any other man on the railroad crew.

One day, a salesman came to the railroad workers' camp. He had a steam-powered drill that he swore could outdrill any man. John Henry took up the challenge. He went head to head with the machine. It was a long day, and John Henry worked hard—the other workers cheered him on; they knew he could win. And John Henry did win—he drilled 14 feet to the machine's 9. But with the race won, he collapsed, and died shortly afterward. John Henry died a steel-driving man, with his hammer still in his hand.

5 This passage is an example of which of the following?

A legend

B fairy tale

C fable

D myth

6 In the space below, explain the reason for your answer to question 5. Include details from the passage.

_____

_____

_____

_____

Performance Indicator: R.2.f

CHAPTER 9

Analyzing Fiction
Lesson 31: Plot

Plot is what happens in a story. The plot explains why things happen and how each event in a story affects the next event. Most of the action in a story relates to the plot, and all of the main characters are somehow involved in the plot. Plot has four main parts, each leading to the next. These parts are summarized below:

- **Conflict:** The struggle or problem faced by the characters in a story.
- **Rising Action:** The events that unfold as part of the conflict.
- **Climax:** The point at which the conflict is addressed by the main character(s); the most exciting part of the story.
- **Resolution:** How the conflict is resolved.

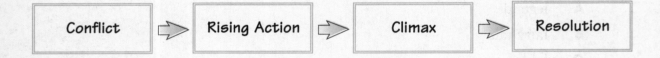

Most stories include all of the elements of plot, though some of the elements may be brief. Each element leads to the next phase of the story—to the next element of plot. Conflict might be a single person trying to overcome some problem, two or more people or groups fighting to win, or any other type of struggle or problem faced by the characters in a story. Generally, conflict is expressed in terms of something vs. something else, or opposition. For example, in the story of the three little pigs and the big bad wolf, the conflict is the desire of the wolf to eat versus (or against) the desire of the pigs not to be eaten.

To determine the conflict in a story, you need to read the story and understand what is going on. Sometimes the conflict will be easy to see, such as in the case of the three little pigs, and other times you will need to look deeper. You should identify the relationships between different characters and determine whether they are working together toward the same goal or rivals competing for something. When you understand who the characters are, you are better able to understand what the conflict of the story is.

Rising action is all of the events that occur as the conflict develops.

Rising action takes up the largest part of the plot. Rising action leads to the climax, which is the turning point in the story. This is often a point of dramatic tension, and the story's most exciting part.

Resolution is the way in which the conflict ends, or is resolved. Generally, one side wins out over the other or some form of compromise, or agreement, is reached. In the story of the three little pigs, the resolution is that the pigs defeat the wolf, and they get to live. The resolution of a story is not only how the story ends, but also how the conflict is resolved and what happens to the characters *after* the climax.

NOTICE: Photocopying any part of this book is forbidden by law.

223

Read the passage below, then answer the question that follows.

Joan was planning a ski trip for the weekend. She was really looking forward to getting away for a few days with her friends and enjoying the snowy beauty of the mountains. Then, two days before they were due to leave, Joan slipped on some ice and broke her wrist. She was incredibly disappointed that she would have to miss the ski trip after all. Then her friend Julie called and convinced her to come along anyway, even if she didn't ski.

What is the conflict in this passage?

_____

_____

_____

 HINT What problem does Joan face?

Example 1

1 **What element of the plot includes the most exciting part of the story?**

A rising action

B conflict

C climax

D resolution

Look back at the elements of plot for clues to help you.

Example 2

It was Sunday afternoon, and for Charlie that meant only one thing: time to wash the dog. It was Charlie's job to give Scruffy a bath every week, and every week, Scruffy would do his best to keep Charlie from succeeding. When he heard the water being run in the bathtub, Scruffy would run and hide under the bed, way back in the far corner where Charlie could not reach him. Eventually, Charlie would have to lift the mattress off the bed to get to the dog, who would usually try to scoot away. If he was lucky, Charlie would be able to grab him before he got away, but even then, Scruffy would wiggle and squirm and fight back with all his strength to avoid being dipped into the water.

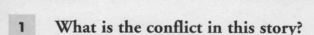

1 **What is the conflict in this story?**

F Charlie vs. the bath

G Charlie vs. Scruffy

H Scruffy vs. Scruffy

J Charlie vs. the bed

What struggle does Charlie face in the passage?

Example 3

Kavi and his mom were walking along the promenade in Brooklyn. They had visited his uncle Remo in Boerum Hill, and had lunch. Now they were strolling before they got back on the subway. They sat on a bench for a few moments in the afternoon sun. Kavi leaned back and closed his eyes. He loved the city. He and his mom came in and visited Uncle Remo once a month. Kavi always brought his homework along and did it on the train. Suddenly he sat up. He had left his backpack at Uncle Remo's! He told his mother, and after a sigh, she got up, and suggested that they walk back over and see if Uncle Remo was still there. Kavi enjoyed the sights as they walked east together along Atlantic Avenue.

3 **Describe the resolution in this story in the space below.**

_____

_____

_____

_____

_____

_____

Discuss your answer with your teacher or class.

Lesson 32
Character

Characters are the people a story is about. Actually, the characters can be animals, fairies, other creatures, or even objects. A story will always have at least one character, although most have more than one.

Writers use **characterization**—the development of characters in a story—to help the reader understand who the characters are, why they behave the way they do, what they believe, and so on. Characterization makes the characters in a story resemble real people, and this makes the story seem more real.

Tools to Create Character

- how the character is described by the narrator
- how the character is described by other characters
- how the character acts
- the character's motivations
- the character's thoughts and words

Read the passage below, then answer the question that follows.

Jason wandered into the kitchen and opened the fridge. He was still looking when his brother came in.

"What are you doing in there, Jason?" asked Marty.

"Nothing, just looking for a snack," said Jason, lazily.

"Mom and Dad will be home in a few minutes, and it was your turn to do the salad for dinner. You better get started."

Jason stepped away from the fridge and let it shut behind him. He gave his brother a hard look as he left the kitchen.

Can you tell anything about these two characters from this passage?

_____

_____

_____

 How do the brothers interact? How do they speak to each other?

The narrator may describe the characters in a story, and may use very specific terms. In some stories you will know what the main characters look like, how they dress, what they like to eat, what their bedrooms look like. In other stories, the characters may not be described at all. If any description is provided, pay attention, and try to see how it reflects on the character. What might it say about a character whose closet is very well ordered, or whose room is a shrine to their favorite band? Descriptive details such as these can help you understand the characters in a story.

Additional descriptive information might be provided by other characters in the story. One character might comment on another's messy appearance or his or her need to be more responsible, for example. What characters say or think about one another can give you information on both characters—after all, what kind of person tells another person that he or she is messy?

Character traits show the reader what a character is like. A person might be generous or stingy, easygoing or nervous, gentle or rough, weak or strong. Sometimes the author tells you directly what a character's traits are. For example, "Jamar is a neat freak." Sometimes, the author simply shows you what a character does and leaves you to figure out on your own what he or she is like as a person. Read the passage on the following page.

Read the passage below, then answer the question that follows.

Jamar sat down on the sofa to watch his favorite show. He heard a crunch as he shifted on the sofa, and when he looked down—how disgusting! There were pieces of potato chips scattered across the sofa, and the bag was peeking out from underneath the coffee table. Jamar got up and brushed off his pants. Then he went to the kitchen for the dust buster. He was going to enjoy his show!

Can you tell anything about Jamar from this passage?

_____

_____

_____

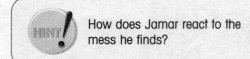 How does Jamar react to the mess he finds?

In this example, the author doesn't say, "Jamar is a neat freak," but you can figure it out from his actions: how disgusted he is by the mess and his immediate action to clean it up.

A character trait can affect a character's actions in the story. If Jamar were less concerned about the mess, he might have simply brushed some of the chips on the floor and turned on the TV. The actions, gestures, and expressions of characters give the reader clues about them. For example, a very confident and outgoing person might make broad, aggressive movements, whereas a shy character might hesitate more or keep his head down when meeting people.

Like a character's traits, a character's feelings can affect what happens in the story. Jamar may not always be a neat-freak; maybe he can't stand potato chips. The reader is given clues about his feelings from his actions. A character's feelings are less general than traits; instead they're more specific to what's happening in the story. You may be generally well-organized and patient, but on certain days, you might feel happier or sadder, more or less fond of your sister, and so on.

What are character motivations? Motivations are what a character wants or desires. Jamar wants to watch his favorite show. Motivations, like traits or feelings, are sometimes spelled out clearly by the author and sometimes not. The author might state that Jamar wants to watch his favorite show, or the author could show Jamar's motivation. Jamar might be described as eagerly turning on the television and smiling widely as his favorite show appears on screen.

Speech, or **dialogue**, is another tool used by writers to bring their characters to life. Dialogue between characters can provide the reader with information about them and their relationship (do they genuinely like one another, are they enemies, etc.). Background about characters may also be revealed through dialogue.

How characters speak—the words they use and how they say them—is called **dialect**. Dialect can tell you things about characters' personal backgrounds. An accent, for example, can indicate that a character comes from a certain part of the world. Very proper grammar may suggest that the character is well-educated. Pay attention to these small clues as you read.

Example 1

Kavi was making faces at Yoshe when Mrs. Lightbear turned around.

"Kavi," she said. "I believe you have work to do."

"Yes, Mrs. Lightbear," said Kavi, smiling. Mrs. Lightbear turned back to the blackboard, and Kavi immediately resumed making faces at Yoshe. She glanced up at him, her cheeks glowing red.

1a **Which of the following BEST describes Kavi?**

A angry

B playful

C anxious

D tired

What do Kavi's actions tell you about him? What motivates him in this passage?

1b **Yoshe's cheeks are red because**

F she has clown makeup on

G she is really hot

H she has a rash

J she is embarrassed

How does Yoshe seem to feel about Kavi's behavior?

Example 2

"Well, I don't mind if I do," said Mona, helping herself to another piece of chocolate. It was her fourth piece. She loved chocolate, and it was so good. She had promised to save her little brother a piece, but within a few more minutes, she found that every piece of chocolate in the box was gone. Mona didn't feel so well. She wiped her chocolatey fingers on her pants, and put the box of chocolates back on the kitchen counter. A whole box of chocolates before dinner! And she had broken her promise to her brother. If her parents found out, she'd be in trouble. Oh, she really didn't feel well.

2a Which of the following BEST describes Mona's behavior?

A   hungry

B   greedy

C   unwell

D   energetic

What does Mona do, and why?

2b Mona's feelings can BEST be described as

F   lonely

G   angry

H   guilty

J   shy

Discuss your answer with your teacher or class.

Lesson 33
Setting

Every story has a **setting**, or where and when the story takes place. Some stories will have very specific settings (an early morning yoga class in Willow Tree Yoga Studio), while others will be more general (Hudson Valley). When a story takes place could be as specific as a time of day or as general as a time period, such as the 50s. The setting might be stated directly, or you might have to determine the setting from clues in the story. The setting may also change as the story unfolds.

 Read the passage below, then answer the question that follows.

Lila stepped up to the counter. It was almost her turn to order. She looked in the glass case at all the flavors. Which one would she choose?

What is the setting of this passage?

_____

_____

_____

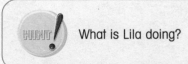 What is Lila doing?

Primary Elements of Setting

- the physical location of the story
- the time period in which the story takes place
- the society and/or customs of the people in the time period in which the story takes place

The easiest part of setting to determine is usually the physical location of the story. In most stories, the narrator identifies early on where the story takes place, or at least provides enough clues for the reader to understand where the characters are. Sometimes the narrator makes the location very clear, providing place names or more general names. In some stories, you will have to pay attention to the clues in the story to figure out its location.

The author may provide dates or very specific clues to help the reader figure out when the events of the story are happening. Language is one clue. People use different terms in different time periods. The slang of the 1940s and 50s is different than the slang used today. For example, if a character really liked someone fifty years ago, he or she might say that someone was "the cat's pajamas" or the "bee's knees." A character in a modern story would not likely say that. Think about the type of language characters use and what time period they would most likely use it in.

Another clue about the time period of a passage is references to historical events. Characters may make references to "the war" or may even name a leader who is currently in power. These comments are especially useful in determining when a story takes place. For example, a character who calls John F. Kennedy "the new president" dates the story in the early 1960s.

A final clue about the time period of a story is culture. The traditions, practices, and customs observed by the characters in a story can help you determine when and where the story takes place. If a character is hooked up to a "time travel machine," the story likely takes place in the future. If two knights are about to battle each other, the story probably takes place in the distant past.

NOTICE: Photocopying any part of this book is forbidden by law.

235

Example 1

The game was going pretty well, but Yoshe was feeling tired. She watched as the ball was passed down the field from teammate to teammate, and knew that soon it would be hers. She looked over at the goal and saw a wide-open path. No one was there, aside from the goalie. She signaled her teammate and sprinted through the grass as the ball bounded toward her. She carried it closer to the goal, and then, with her back to the goalie, gave the ball a solid kick. It soared up and then hit the ground, bouncing into the net between the stunned goalie's legs.

1 **What is the setting of this passage?**

A inside a gymnasium

B in a classroom

C on a field

D at Yoshe's house

What clues about setting are there in the passage?

Example 2

Horns were beeping all around. Martine could hardly hear herself think. She rolled the window up, to keep out the blaring sounds, but she looked out the window. There were tall buildings all around, and from her perspective, she couldn't catch even a glimpse of the sky. It looked overcast, anyway. She sighed, and leaned back against her seat, trying to will herself to have patience.

2 **This passage MOST LIKELY takes place in**

F   a car in traffic in a city

G   a boat on the harbor

H   a tall building in the city

J   a suburban neighborhood

SELF Coach™   Discuss your answer with your teacher or class.

Performance Indicators: R.2.i, W.2.d

Lesson 34
Theme

Theme refers to the central idea or meaning of a selection. It is the general idea or insight about life that an author wants the reader to understand. Theme differs from plot in that the plot of a story is the events and what happens to specific characters, while theme refers to the *general message* of the story.

A written work may have a single theme or several themes. A story theme might be something like

> *Bad things happen to good people.*

In such a story, you might have a character who is respected and loved by everyone for his or her good deeds, hard work, and charitable nature. Or there might be a group of several good people who have bad things happen to them, even though the reader believes they should not.

Another theme might be

> *Money does not buy happiness.*

A story with this theme might revolve around a person with a lot of money, property, luxury items, etc., but who lives a lonely life or is surrounded by people who care only about his or her money.

The author usually does not tell the reader what the theme of a story is. Rather, you have to figure it out for yourself. To do so, try to determine the main focus of the story, and how it applies to life in general. Ask yourself, "What lesson should I take from this passage?"

Common Literary Themes

- **bravery**—courage in the face of real or perceived danger
- **loyalty**—being faithful
- **friendship**—often involves valuing a relationship over personal gain
- **loneliness**—often involves the pain related to being on one's own
- **love**—caring for another person, often even more than oneself
- **greed**—valuing objects and riches over all else

Remember that the theme of a story is a major idea, broad enough to cover the entire scope of a literary work. Smaller ideas within the story are not likely to be the story's theme.

The best way to identify the theme of a story is to consider the actions, thoughts, and words of characters, and think about their greater meaning, or the effect they have on the outcome of the story. When a certain idea or belief, such as bravery, is repeated throughout the course of a story, you can generally determine that it relates to the theme.

Example 1

Jamar was worried about his piano recital. He had practiced his piece for weeks, and now it was finally the day of the concert. What if he made a fool of himself? Maybe he would forget how to play the piano entirely. He had practiced an hour that afternoon, just to ease his mind. When the time came for him to perform that evening, all of his hard work paid off. He played beautifully and felt great about the concert.

1 **What is the theme of this passage?**

A Be careful what you wish for.

B Hard work pays off.

C Music adds joy to life.

D Worry gets you nowhere.

Discuss your answer with your teacher or class.

Lesson 35
Comparing Literary Elements

Comparing the elements in stories can help you to learn more about those elements. This lesson will teach you how to compare and contrast characters, settings, and themes.

Character

One of your jobs as a reader is to compare and contrast the characters of a story. When you read, you do some automatic comparing and contrasting in your head to keep track of the characters you are reading about. There are many different aspects of characters that you can compare and contrast, including age and behavior.

Character Points to Compare

- age (young or old)
- physical appearance (pale, skinny, handsome)
- physical status (weak, athletic, limping)
- personality traits (shy, loving, nervous)
- nationality (American, Nigerian)
- profession (accountant, student, fisherman)
- marital status (single, divorced, married)
- family status (mother, child, uncle)

Example 1

Lorelai and Sue had been best friends since Sue moved to Hastings in first grade. The girls were like sisters. They lived on the same block and went to the same school. Both loved Chinese food and swimming and adventure stories. The one thing that they could not do was share clothes. Sue was short and athletic, and Lorelai was tall and thin. Once for a sleepover, Lorelai had worn one of Sue's nightshirts, and it had fit her almost like a normal t-shirt.

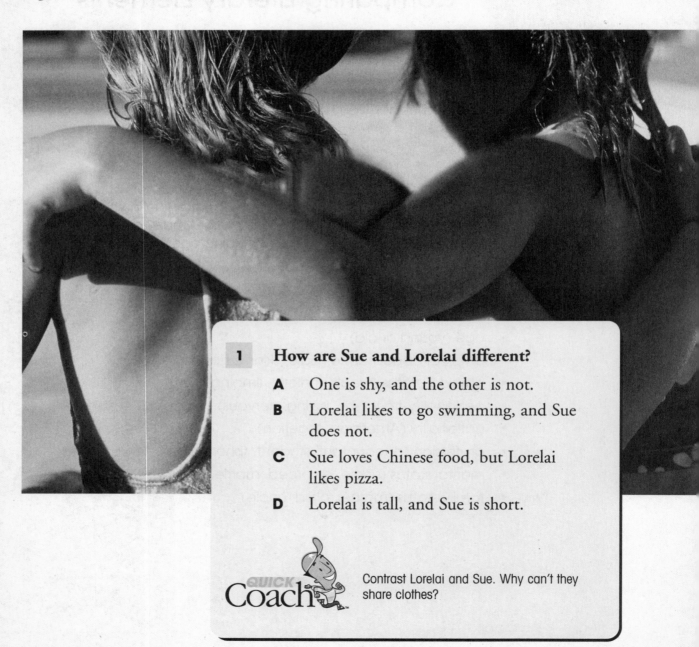

1 **How are Sue and Lorelai different?**

A One is shy, and the other is not.

B Lorelai likes to go swimming, and Sue does not.

C Sue loves Chinese food, but Lorelai likes pizza.

D Lorelai is tall, and Sue is short.

QUICK Coach™

Contrast Lorelai and Sue. Why can't they share clothes?

Setting

Just as you can compare characters, you can also compare settings. Sometimes the setting of a story or play will change, and you will be able to compare settings within a single literary work. You can also compare settings in two or more literary works. You might be asked to compare settings in texts set in the same location, but in different time periods. The settings will have many similarities, but will also have differences, both physical and cultural.

 Read the passage below, then answer the question that follows.

When he was 7, Roberto had spent the summer in Tucson with cousins. They had spent their mornings outside playing, and then in the hot afternoon sun, they came inside for lunch and a siesta. Sometimes, Roberto would spend the afternoon with his tía Josefa, helping her to make fresh corn tamales or carne asada. She spent hours preparing these special foods for the family, and Roberto paid close attention, knowing that this was his chance to learn. Now, back in Queens, he sometimes found himself hungry for those tender tamales with cheese and peppers, and on a summer afternoon, he would go to the market with his father for the ingredients. They'd return to their apartment, where Roberto would spend several hours alone in the small kitchen preparing the tamales. Roberto didn't think they ever tasted as good as Tía Josefa's, but he and his parents enjoyed them anyhow. He thought that he might need to be at a table crowded with cousins for the tamales to taste as good.

Compare the settings within this passage.

_____

_____

_____

_____

 Is there more than one setting in the passage? How are they similar? How are they different?

Remember the aspects of setting from Lesson 33? Review them when comparing setting in literary works.

Theme

It's also possible to compare themes within literary works. Sometimes, you may be asked to compare the themes from two or more stories. To do this, you need to decide what the central message(s) or idea(s) are in each story—remember, there may be more than one theme in a story. Once you've figured out what some of the themes are, decide how the main theme from each story is similar to and different from the themes of the other stories.

The chart below compares two stories.

"The Bracelet"	"Amy's Promise"
• Joanne's father gives her a bracelet for her birthday • Joanne takes it off in gym class but does not put it in her locker and loses it • The custodian finds it and returns it • Joanne is more careful with her bracelet in the future	• Amy promises to go to her friend's recital • Amy's cousin offers her tickets to a baseball game on the same day as the recital • Amy tells her friend that she is sick, then goes to the game with her cousin • Amy's friend learns the truth and is very hurt • Amy feels terrible and never lies to her again

How might you compare the themes in this story? Look at the events and the characters' actions. Joanne is careless and loses her bracelet. Amy is thoughtless. She breaks a promise to a friend and lies to her. One possible theme to compare is that one should think more carefully about one's actions. Or that careless actions will produce negative results. But Joanne is more careful after she gets her bracelet back, and Amy feels badly about her actions and never lies to her friend again. So another theme might be that people have the ability to change. Or that something good can come out of something bad. Of course, a major theme that both stories share is one of honesty. The custodian is honest, but at first Amy is not. She learns that honesty is the best policy.

Example 2

1. Cristina's stomach grumbled as she entered the school cafeteria. She was really hungry that day and, naturally, had left the lunch her father had packed for her on the kitchen counter. All she had was 75 cents, just enough to buy a small package of crackers from the vending machine. Cristina selected a corner table and settled in for her sad meal of crackers. It was her first week at a new school and she didn't know anyone well enough to ask to borrow a couple of bucks for lunch. She looked up as a girl she'd seen in science class that morning slid into the chair across from her. "Hi. I'm Nadia," she said. "Did you forget your lunch?" Cristina nodded silently. Nadia smiled. "I've done that a few times. Want to share mine?" Cristina hesitated, then encouraged by Nadia's friendliness, gladly accepted. In a few minutes, each girl was enjoying her half of a chicken sandwich and granola bar. Suddenly, Cristina noticed her dad waving from the doorway, a lunch bag in his hand. Cristina grinned and waved him over. "Now, Nadia, it's my turn to share my lunch with you."

2. Gene walked into the school cafeteria with a smile on his face. He was having a good day. He'd left his lunch home that morning, but a lucky twist of fate had dropped a free lunch practically into his lap. A few minutes ago, he had found someone's forgotten lunch bag in the music room. Gene knew he should have given it to the teacher, in case the student came back, but he couldn't pass up a free lunch. He figured whoever lost it would learn a lesson. It wasn't exactly stealing, just not giving it back. Gene ate the peanut butter sandwich by himself, hoping whoever lost it wouldn't see him. There was also a plastic container with a cream-colored pudding in it. It tasted a bit strange, but not bad enough to pass up. Gene quickly scoffed it down. Suddenly, he noticed Rasheed standing over him, looking confused. "Hey, Gene, is that my lunch?" Gene looked up innocently. "Is it?" he responded. Gene looked more worried than angry. "I was looking for that," Rasheed said, pointing at the empty pudding container. "I don't know how to tell you this, but you just ate my science experiment."

2a **Which of the following would BEST describe the theme of the first passage?**

  A   Be more careful where you leave your lunch.

  B   Good things can happen when you think of others besides yourself.

  C   You won't go wrong if you learn from your mistakes.

  D   A true friend is hard to find.

What kind of person is Nadia?

2b **What is the theme of the second passage, and how does it differ from that of the first passage? Use examples from the passages to support your answer. Use your own paper for your response.**

Discuss your answer with your teacher or class.

Coached Reading

This story is about a girl about to take a trip to Paris. As you read the story, use the statements and questions in the margin to help your understanding.

 Your teacher may read this selection to you.

Michele and her family were taking a trip to Paris. Her mom had to go there for business, and her parents decided to take the whole family. Michele tried to be excited about the trip, but she was apprehensive. She had never flown in an airplane before, or been to a foreign country, and was worried about what might happen there. How would she get along? She didn't speak French.

Michele was a worrier. That's what her dad said. He and her mom had done a lot of traveling before Michele and her brother were born, and they were comfortable with going anywhere. Michele thought she would describe herself as a homebody. She wasn't opposed to travel itself, but there was no place she really wanted to go. She was happy at home, near her favorite ice cream place, Italian restaurant, and library. Here she had her friends, her room, her cat, Zelda. She didn't really *want* to go to Paris.

What can you tell about Michele so far?

"We're only going for two weeks, Michele. You just need to relax. It's going to be really great. Think about it—the Eiffel Tower, the Louvre, real French fries! We'll have a great time. Even you will," said her brother, Zachary.

Michele ignored him. She ignored them all, until the night before they were to leave. Mom had the passports and tickets and was getting the bags organized. Grandma was coming over to pick up Zelda. Dad was leaving a key with the neighbor for the mail. Zachary was at his friend Kevin's house, leaving his Guinea pig Miguel there. And Michele? She hadn't finished packing, and she sat in a chair in her room, clothes everywhere, with Zelda on her lap. She heard the doorbell, and then voices downstairs. Soon footsteps were coming down the hall, and then Grandma stood in front of her door.

"Hi, Shelly," said Grandma, smiling. "I've come to get my boarder."

"Maybe you can have two boarders, Grandma," said Michele.

"Why? Zach's friend can't keep that Guinea pig? I told him I'd keep it for him," said Grandma.

"No, not Miguel," said Michele, her eyes welling. "Me."

"You!" said Grandma, surprised. "Why would you need to come stay with me? What's happened?"

"Nothing—really," stammered Michele. "I just don't want to go to Paris. Zachary thinks the whole thing will be fun, but I don't. I like it here. I don't want to eat French food and speak French and ride a plane."

How are Michele and her brother similar? How are they different?

What part of the plot takes place in this section of the passage?

"Well, Shelly," said Grandma, sitting on Michele's bed, "you really need to go. You're doing yourself and your family a disservice if you don't go. You have to be willing to try new things, Shelly. If you don't, you'll miss out on being the best you can be in this world." She smiled at Michele. "I was 21 when I left home and moved to New York with my friend May. I didn't think I wanted to go, but she convinced me to give it a try. I promised her one month. If I didn't like it, I would go home."

"What happened?" asked Michele, no longer thinking about Paris.

"Two weeks after I got there, I met Granddad at a dinner party. He worked for the state department and was going to Japan in three weeks. A week before he left, we were married, and I moved to Japan, instead of back home. I wouldn't trade those years for the world. I discovered I'm a very capable person, in Japan, Shel."

"What would have happened if you never went to New York?" asked Michele.

"I'd be in Grand Rapids, I guess," said Grandma. "I'm sure I'd have had a nice life. But not this one."

Michele brought Zelda over and put her in Grandma's lap. "Grandma," she said, smiling, "help me pack?"

What is the setting of the passage?

What is the theme of the passage?

Re-read the story, and ask yourself the questions in the margin again. Then answer questions 1 through 4.

1 **This story is set**

   A   in a school

   B   in New York

   C   in Paris

   D   in a bedroom

2 **The theme of the story is likely**

   F   Paris is a lot of fun

   G   it's nice to stay at home sometimes

   H   it's good to try new things

   J   kids have to do what their parents say

3 **Briefly describe the conflict in the story.**

_____

_____

_____

4 **Briefly compare Michele and her grandmother. What are their similarities? Their differences?**

_____

_____

_____

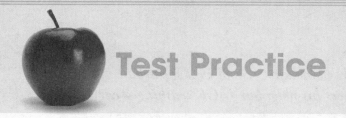

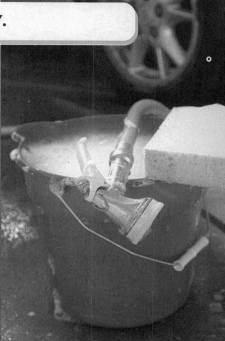

Read this story and drama. Then answer questions 1 through 7.

1. Eli was walking home from school with Rebecca when he saw Jack Spurlitzer out in his driveway. Jack was in high school, and Eli wanted Jack to like him. He sometimes imagined that Jack was his big brother, and that they did lots of stuff together. Jack would play catch with him and teach him all about cars. They would go to the movies together and camping, too. Then he snapped out of it. He remembered that what he had was Rebecca, a sister who didn't much like hanging out with him at all. Rebecca called him Eely, which she thought was funny. They never had fun together. Jack was different. They were about to pass him— Eli worked up his courage. Could he try to speak with him?

"Hey, Jack," he said, as casually as he could.

Jack looked up from the car he was washing. "Hey, Eli," said Jack. "What's up?"

"Oh, not much," said Eli. "How about you?"

"Just washing my dad's car. If I don't get my work done, I can't go to the movies, you know?"

"Yeah, I know," said Eli, who really didn't know. But he was having a conversation with Jack. He glanced nervously at the sidewalk and was relieved that Rebecca had continued down the block to their house. "So, what are you going to see?"

"I think we're going to take in that new martial arts movie at the mall," said Jack, still washing the car.

"Yeah, I hear that one's good," said Eli. "I want to see that, too."

"Well, I'll let you know how it is," said Jack, smiling.

"I might go with my dad tonight or tomorrow," lied Eli. "So maybe I'll see you there."

"Okay," smiled Jack. "Have a good weekend, Eli."

"You, too, Jack," said Eli. He stood a few seconds, watching Jack, and then he turned and went home, smiling the whole way.

2. Scene 1

Outside, a hot spring afternoon. ELI walks home after school in a suburban neighborhood. He strolls distractedly and sees his neighbor JACK washing a car in his driveway.

ELI   *[casually]* Hey, Jack, how ya doin'?

JACK   *[looks up from the car]* I'm good. *[goes back to washing car, ignores ELI]*

ELI   So, what's up?

JACK   I'm washing my dad's car.

ELI   Right. Nice car. *[desperate now]* So. Have you seen the new martial arts movie at the Cineplex?

JACK   No. I'm going tonight.

ELI   Hey, me too. Maybe I'll see you there! *[JACK continues to wash the car, ignoring ELI]*

           Okay, well, see you around, I guess. *[JACK doesn't respond. ELI strolls off, hands in pockets, looking dejected]*

[ELI is halfway down the block. JACK looks up and watches him walk away. Smirks, and goes back to washing the car.]

1 Which of the following **best** describes Eli in the story?

A angry

B confused

C sincere

D insincere

2 What is the setting of the drama?

F outside on a spring afternoon

G a summer morning

H morning on a school day

J a schoolyard

3 Which of the following **best** describes Eli's conflict in the story?

A Eli wants to go to the movies with Jack.

B Eli is late for school but wants to talk to Jack.

C Eli wants to talk to Jack but is very nervous.

D Eli wants Jack to invite him over.

4 Briefly compare the character Jack as he appears in the story and as he appears in the drama. Are the characters similar? What are their differences? Cite evidence from the passage to support your answer.

_____

_____

_____

_____

5   Which of the following **best** describes the theme of the story?

   F   Lying will get you nowhere.

   G   When at first you don't succeed, try again.

   H   Don't confuse your neighbors with your friends.

   J   Don't let your fears stop you from doing things.

6   Are the themes in the story and the drama similar? Explain your answer in the space below.

_____

_____

_____

_____

7   Compare the setting in the story and the drama. What clues about the setting can you find in each passage? Cite examples in your answer.

_____

_____

_____

_____

_____

CHAPTER 10

Literary Techniques

Lesson 36: Metaphor and Simile

Words and phrases can have two types of meanings: literal and figurative. The **literal meaning** of a word or phrase is its exact, specific meaning. This meaning is taken at face value, so no interpretation is needed. The **figurative meaning** of a word is a more imaginative, creative interpretation. When writers use figurative language, they do not literally mean what they say. Writers use figurative language to make their writing more expressive and colorful.

Metaphor

A **metaphor** is a figure of speech that expresses an idea through the image of another object. Metaphors are implied comparisons, meaning that they are not directly identified, and the comparison is not meant literally.

Generally, metaphors use a form of the verb *to be*, such as *is* and *are*.

> George is a pig.

In this sentence, the writer creates a metaphor comparing George to a pig, although it is not clear exactly how George is like a pig. Most likely, the writer means that, like a pig, George is messy and sloppy.

> Loren was a shimmering beacon in the night.

In this sentence, Loren is compared to a shimmering beacon in the night. To figure out what the writer is trying to say, you must first figure out what a "shimmering beacon in the night" is. A beacon is a type of light used to guide ships in the darkness. In this sense, then, the writer is saying that Loren is an invaluable guide that helps the writer to find his way through life during a difficult time. Some metaphors are easy to understand, and some require more thought.

Examples of Metaphors

- These biscuits are rocks.
- Paul is a diamond in the rough.
- Raymond is a bear when he's tired.
- While the rest of the family was falling apart, Bridget remained a rock.
- After the accident, Jason was a wreck.

 Read the passage below, then answer the question that follows.

"Can I borrow your glue?" Jane asked sweetly, poking her head into her brother's room.

"No," replied James. "It's my glue, and you'll mess it up. Go get your own."

"You're such a scrooge," said Jane, before leaving.

What is the metaphor in this passage?

_____

_____

_____

 Is something or someone compared to something else in this passage?

Example 1

Martine and her cousin Jessie were in Martine's room. Martine was doing her homework. Jessie was sitting on Martine's bed, flipping through a magazine.

"Let's do something, Martine," pleaded Jessie.

"Like what?" asked Martine.

"Like anything," said Jessie. "Let's go swimming in the river by Eddie's house."

"That's dangerous," said Martine. "Besides, I have homework to do."

"You're such a stick in the mud," said Jessie, with a sigh.

1 **Which sentence from the passage contains a metaphor?**

A "Let's go swimming in the river by Eddie's house."

B "You're such a stick in the mud."

C "Jessie was sitting on Martine's bed, flipping through a magazine."

D "Besides, I have homework to do."

Remember that a metaphor often uses a form of the verb "to be" and compares things or people to something else.

Similes

Like metaphors, **similes** compare two unlike things, but similes use either *as* or *like* to connect the words being compared. When you use a simile to make a comparison, you create an image in the reader's mind that connects qualities of the two items you are comparing. For example:

> The child was as quiet as a mouse.

The person writing this sentence does not *literally* mean that the child only made high-pitched squeaks from time to time. Instead, the writer is saying that the child made very little noise, just as a mouse makes very little noise.

As with metaphors, the comparison drawn in a simile is often an exaggeration. For example:

> John was as cold as ice.

In this sentence, John is compared to the temperature of ice. John is not *literally* the temperature of ice. This is an exaggeration to make a point. This comparison may indicate that John has a cold attitude or that he is very cold. The context of the sentence—the other sentences in the passage—will help you understand the meaning of the comparison.

When you read, remember that a sentence is not automatically a simile because it includes *like* or *as*. The sentence must *compare* two different things.

 THINKING IT THROUGH Read the passage below, then answer the question that follows.

Evan settled into the starting position for the 100-meter dash. Tuning out the cheering crowd, Evan pictured himself crossing the finish line. He tried not to think of the other runners kneeling on either side of him. Evan focused on his own breathing and the power that flowed through his legs. A cheetah ready to sprint, Evan waited for the signal. The finish line loomed ahead like a pot of gold at the end of a rainbow.

What is the simile in this passage?

_____

_____

_____

 HINT! Is there a comparison that uses "like" or "as" in this passage?

Example 2

Jamar was camping out with his uncle Steffan. They had put the tent up, and were sitting around the campfire, toasting marshmallows. It had been a busy day. Jamar felt like he could eat a dozen marshmallows. Jamar put his head back and looked up at the vast sky. He saw stars, twinkling like diamonds across the sky.

2 **Which sentence from the passage includes a simile?**

F "Jamar felt like he could eat a dozen marshmallows."

G "Jamar was camping out with his uncle Steffan."

H "Jamar put his head back and looked up at the vast sky."

J "He saw stars, twinkling like diamonds across the sky.

QUICK
Coach™

Only one of these sentences uses "like" or "as" to compare two different things.

Example 3

3 **Which sentence includes a simile?**

A Julie thought she might like an apple.

B As I was saying, we should not throw rocks at each other.

C She sings like an angel.

D His was blue, and mine was green.

Only one of the sentences uses "like" or "as" to compare two different things.

Example 4

4 **Which simile would you use to indicate that something was slow?**

F like a hyena

G like a flash

H as a cat

J as a snail

Discuss your answer with your teacher or class.

Lesson 37
Symbolism

Symbolism is a literary device that uses one object to represent, or stand for, something else. The object is usually concrete, or real, and it represents something abstract, such as an idea or a feeling. When something acts as a symbol, some aspect of the item and its qualities is applied to something else. For example, a sunset might symbolize the end of something, just as it literally indicates the end of the day. If a person is said to have a "heart of stone," the heart symbolizes love and affection, while stone symbolizes coldness and an inability to change. Therefore, the term "heart of stone" means that the person is unfeeling and uncaring, just as a stone would be.

Symbol	What It Symbolizes
clouds	confusion, despair
dove	peace
water	life
clock	passage of time
baby	new beginning
spring	new beginning
winter	something coming to a close or old age
rain	sadness, sorrow, negativity
rainbow	hope, better times
eagle	liberty, freedom
seedling	hope

Often the symbol an author uses will be common and easy to recognize. A dove might stand for peace, or an eagle might symbolize liberty. Authors may also use less common symbols, or they might create their own. A writer might use an empty house to symbolize loneliness, for example.

If an object appears in a story more than once, you should consider what it might represent, other than its literal meaning. When and where does the object appear? Does it have some significance to a character in the story? Answering these questions can help you determine what an object symbolizes. Remember that a writer can choose to make any object symbolic, and your job as a reader is to discover the hidden, symbolic meanings placed in the story by the writer.

 Read the passage below, then answer the question that follows.

Risa awoke at 7:00 AM with a grin on her face. After two months out of work, she had finally found the perfect job. She would be doing what she had always wanted to do and earning more money than she'd earned in her entire life. She felt as if this was the start of a new life for her.

Risa stretched and climbed out of bed. She stuck her head out of her bedroom window and breathed in the morning air. It was a beautiful spring day. Her neighbor, Mrs. Hewitt, was attending to her rose garden. A squirrel scampered up a nearby oak tree and bounced off a branch. Risa smiled and nodded to herself. It was going to be a good day.

What is the symbolism in this passage?

_____

_____

_____

_____

 How does Risa feel and why?

Example 1

The prisoners of war had been locked in the POW camp for months now, and conditions were only getting worse. They had hoped that the army would have arrived by now to free them, but they had not seen or heard of any friendly forces in the area. In a prison, sometimes only the hope of freedom can keep you going, and these men were giving in to despair. Then one man found a crumpled piece of paper. He flattened it out and began folding it carefully. A fold here, a seam there, until finally he had fashioned a fine paper airplane. Others gathered around him as he walked directly up to the fence. For a moment, they seemed to forget where they were. Some argued over whether the plane would make it. Others waited silently to see what would happen. The man took a stance before the fence, aimed the plane carefully, and then let it fly. It fell, as did the men's spirits. But he picked it up and tried again. And he failed again.

For nearly an hour, he repeatedly threw the plane and then went to recover it as it failed to clear the fence. Some men walked away, though most did not. Trying yet again, the man threw the plane toward the fence, and this time it caught a breeze. It sailed gracefully up and over the fence, with the wind carrying it right to the edge of the forest. The men laughed and cheered and talked about that plane for the rest of the day. That night the ghost of despair had been defeated.

1 **What did the flight of the paper airplane symbolize?**

A freedom

B hunger

C imprisonment

D joy

Where does the airplane go? What might this mean to someone in a prison?

Performance Indicators: R.2.g, L.2.c

Lesson 38
Personification

Another type of language with figurative meaning is personification. **Personification** is when a writer gives human qualities to animals and objects. For example, when an author writes, "My homework stared at me while I watched television," he does not mean that his homework actually has eyes. He is using personification to help make his writing more descriptive and interesting to read.

This poem contains several examples of personification.

> Hey diddle diddle,
> The cat played the fiddle,
> The cow jumped over the moon,
> The little dog laughed to see such sport,
> And the dish ran away with the spoon.

Cats cannot really play musical instruments, dogs do not really laugh, and dishes and spoons cannot run. These are all examples of personification because they tell you that non-human things are doing things only real people can do. Personification makes the animals and objects in this poem come to life as characters.

THINKING IT THROUGH Read the passage below, then answer the question that follows.

Shadi sat on his bed, reading a book. Just as he was about to turn the page, his pillow said, "Hey, I'm not done reading that yet!"

"Oh, leave him alone!" the dresser said. "It's his book, not yours!"

"If he is going to sleep on me, then I should be allowed to read his book!" the pillow argued back.

Shadi was amazed by what was happening. Then he heard a buzzing noise. He opened his eyes and realized that he had been sleeping. It was all a dream!

What is one example of personification in this passage?

_____

_____

_____

 HINT! People are the only creatures that can really talk.

Example 1

Luis and his family hopped out of the car, armed with beach bags, towels, and pails. As they got closer to the beach, Luis saw the sun's rays dancing on the waves. He couldn't wait to go for a swim! Luis threw his towel on the sand and ran to the edge of the ocean. He put his feet in the water to test the temperature. It was cold at first, but after a minute, he was ready to dive in. Luis swam out a short distance then turned over on his back to float on top of the waves. As he looked up at the sunny sky, he thought, "What a perfect day!"

1 **Which phrase from the passage shows personification?**

A threw his towel

B sun's rays dancing

C go for a swim

D put his feet in

 **SELF Coach** Discuss your answer with your teacher or class.

Performance Indicators: R.2.g, L.2.c

Lesson 39
Foreshadowing

Sometimes, you can tell when the parts of plot—like climax—are going to happen, or how they will work out. How? With a type of clue, or hint, called **foreshadowing**. Foreshadowing helps tell you what's going to happen, without being too obvious.

Foreshadowing involves providing clues to the reader to suggest future events. This means that the writer will give the reader hints about what will happen later in the story, often through the comments of a character or some seemingly unrelated event. For example, one character might tell another, "I never fly—I have a terrible fear of heights." Then later in the story, that character must test his fear of heights. By having the first character tell the second character about his fear, the writer is foreshadowing later events in the story.

Sometimes symbolism is used to foreshadow future events. The sky may darken to hint at trouble, for example. Or a character may see a rainbow and then have good luck.

Read the passage below, then answer the question that follows.

Arlo was on the porch when the sun went behind the clouds. The sky darkened, and Arlo knew that something terrible was coming. He waited.

What is foreshadowed in the passage?

_____

_____

_____

 What is hinted at or predicted?

Foreshadowing creates certain expectations in the reader, and helps build suspense in the story until the reader can see if what was hinted at actually happens—foreshadowing is not always accurate. It can be used to throw readers off the actual events of the story. (Mystery writers often use this technique.) Often, a reader won't realize there was foreshadowing in the story until after the story is finished. Then, looking back, the reader may be able to find clues about how the story would turn out.

Example 1

Esme walked inside, and went to the kitchen for more lemonade. It was a beautiful day, perfect for gardening, which Esme really needed to catch up on. The kids were at their grandmother's house, and Esme had the day to herself. She would have enjoyed the day even more, but she could not shake the feeling that something was wrong. She had been forcing herself not to call and check on the kids, but didn't know if she could wait any longer. She felt it in her gut: something was wrong. She poured the lemonade and went to pick up the phone. Before she reached it, the phone began to ring.

1 What is foreshadowed in this passage?

- **A** Esme has a lot of gardening to do.

- **B** Esme doesn't feel well.

- **C** Something is wrong, maybe with Esme's kids.

- **D** The day will get even hotter.

Does the passage suggest any outcome?

Coached Reading

This story is about a girl who has an adventure with an alligator. As you read the story, use the statements and questions in the margin to help your understanding.

 DEAD ALOUD Your teacher may read this selection to you.

My dad grew up on a farm in Florida, and he's full of adventure stories about life there. Some of them, well, they really make it surprising that he made it out of childhood on that farm. This is one of those stories.

There was a pond on the farm, and they used to go fishing in it. One day, my dad's brother, Jerry, saw an alligator in the pond. It was a big alligator, he thought. He told his dad, but they decided to live and let live, so to speak. Would the alligator really abide by that plan? I think I would have made other suggestions. But I wasn't there. Anyway, they all coexisted with the alligator pretty well. They even named him Little Fella, though he wasn't at all little. Little Fella was as happy as a clam in mud, Jerry used to say. Which makes sense, since he was in mud.

Is there a metaphor or simile in this part of the passage?

There were fewer fish in the pond, and they couldn't go swimming in it anymore—that was the biggest loss. Have you ever been to Florida in the summertime? It's just a big wet oven. Hot, hot, hot, and so humid. Then every day, the humidity builds, and a thunderstorm breaks the humidity for 10 or 15 minutes. Then it's hot and humid again. They swam in that pond a lot before Little Fella moved in.

One summer day, they had an alligator adventure. My dad went down to the pond to fish, and saw the alligator lying on the bank. *Maybe he's sunning himself,* thought my dad, though he knew that it was too hot. Gators didn't lie out in the heat of midday like that. It lay there on the bank the whole time he fished. He didn't catch a thing, and then he went and got his brother. Jerry was the brave one, or the crazy one, depending on how you look at it. I look at it like crazy. Jerry came down to the pond, with my dad trailing after him. He walked right up to the gator, and it didn't move. He nudged it with his shoe, and it still didn't move. An alligator can move really fast when it wants to, and my dad thought Jerry would be eaten, for sure. But he wasn't.

"It's dead, Buddy," said Jerry.

"What should we do? Should we call Daddy?"

"It's dead, Buddy. What's Daddy gonna do? Let's just move it out of the sun ourselves."

> What is the foreshadowing in this part of the story?

My dad thought this was crazy, and he said so, but there was no arguing with Jerry. This was a big alligator. Seven feet long. They tied a rope around his neck, and between the two of them, they pulled and pushed him along until he was near the cabin, in the shade. The cabin was a separate little guest house on the farm where my dad's sister, Nancy lived. Nancy was the oldest at home. She was going to college. The oldest got to live in the cabin, was the rule. Uncle Jerry decided they should leave the alligator on Nancy's porch.

"On the porch? Jerry, you're crazy as a loon. Nancy will be scared to death," said my dad.

"That's the idea, Buddy," said Jerry, pulling the gator toward the porch. Nancy was inside the cabin, sleeping in. It was her day off, and she had worked late the night before at the café in town, where she waitressed to pay for school.

So they hauled the alligator onto the porch, and left him there, all seven feet of him. "He looks like he's sleeping," my dad said.

"Have a good rest, Little Fella," said Jerry, patting the gator's tail.

> What literary device is used in this section?

NOTICE: Photocopying any part of this book is forbidden by law.

271

They went back over to the main house and got some lunch, and after about an hour, they heard the shrillest scream! They ran over to the cabin, and got there in time to see that gator clamber down off the porch and head across the yard toward the pond. Nancy stood in the doorway to the little cabin, tears streaming down her face.

"I think she scared him back to life," said Jerry. My dad just stared after that gator, and he stayed away from the pond for a while.

Re-read the story, and ask yourself the questions in the margin again. Then answer questions 1 through 6.

1 Read this sentence from the story.

Would the alligator really abide by that plan?

This sentence is an example of

A symbolism

B personification

C metaphor

D simile

2 Which of the following is an example of metaphor in the story?

F "Little Fella was as happy as a clam in mud."

G "It was a big alligator, he thought."

H "It's just a big wet oven."

J "The oldest got to live in the cabin, was the rule."

3 The alligator may be seen as a symbol of

A how soundly alligators sleep

B how unpredictable nature is

C how friendly alligators are

D why people and alligators don't coexist well

4   **Briefly describe an instance of foreshadowing in the story. Does what it hints at happen in the story?**

_____

_____

_____

_____

_____

5   **Read the following line from the passage.**

Jerry, you're crazy as a loon.

This is an example of which of the following?

F   symbolism

G   foreshadowing

H   simile

J   metaphor

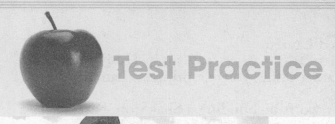

Test Practice

Read this story. Then answer questions 1 through 4.

Lauren walked past the deserted house in her neighborhood. *I wish someone nice would move in there, she thought.* She thought this every time she passed the lonely house. It was older, and looked like a haunted house, her sister would say. Lauren thought it was a lovely house. It was a castle, but it definitely needed a little extra care.

She imagined the former life of the house: glamorous parties, beautifully dressed guests, dancing. The house would have been perfectly painted and landscaped. She really could see it, when she looked at the falling-down old castle. It seemed to her to show a side of the town that had faded away. If a nice family would move in and take care of it, the house would again be beautiful and happy.

She stood a few moments longer and then went home. At dinner that night, she was quite surprised when her mother said that the house had been bought, finally. Someone had bought her castle! Nothing could have interested her more, and she was disappointed that her mother didn't know who bought it or what they planned to do with it.

"They'll move into it, of course, and fix it up and take care of it. It really needs taking care of," said Lauren.

"Right, that's just what it needs," said her sister snidely. "They need to tear it down and build something useful there, like a SnakStop."

"They can't do that to the castle!" cried Lauren.

"The castle!" crowed her sister. "If that's a castle, you're a princess, Lauren."

"Now, girls," said their mother. "They won't be building a SnakStop, because it's a residentially zoned property. Someone will live there, unless they apply to rezone it."

Lauren had never been so happy to have a lawyer for a mother.

---

1 Read this sentence from the story.

> **She thought this every time she passed the lonely house.**

This is an example of

A simile

B metaphor

C personification

D foreshadowing

2 Which of the following sentences from the story contains a simile?

F "It was older, and looked like a haunted house, her sister would say."

G "Lauren thought it was a lovely house."

H "Someone had bought her castle!"

J "The house would have been perfectly painted and landscaped."

3 What does the castle symbolize to Lauren?

A a haunted house

B a happy family life

C the problems in society today

D a time that had faded away

4 List an example of foreshadowing from the story. Does the foreshadowing turn out to be true? Explain your answer using examples from the story.

_____

_____

_____

_____

_____

Read this story about a swim team meet. Then answer questions 5 through 8.

The Oakhurst Lions swim team was ready for this meet. Elliott was the captain of the swim team, and he was most certainly ready—for a big win. Elliot was slick and small, and he looked like a seal in the water. Out of the water, he looked kind of klutzy and uncertain of himself, but the pool loved him. In it, he became something else. He was confident and agile. He was a lion–strong, certain, powerful. This was why Elliott had always loved swimming. In the pool was where he could be himself, but also better than himself—or maybe it was just the best of himself.

He trained every day, swimming laps at the school pool in every season. In the summer, he was a lifeguard at a local pool, and spent much of the day in or around the pool. He could imagine spending his entire life that way, working in or around the pool. He looked out now at the school pool. It was almost time. The pool looked like a magical mirror. There was a mist hanging over it that made it look enchanted, somehow. He half expected to see a unicorn across the pool.

He didn't, of course. He did see his parents sitting in the bleachers. He raised a hand and waved, and his mother waved back, a little too enthusiastically. His teammate Morales brought over the heat sheet, and Elliot looked it over.

They were beginning to line up the heats in the 100-meter freestyle. He had a while before his first event, but was ready to cheer on his teammates. "Remember," he called, "if you're going to lose, lose big!"

5 Which of the following sentences from the passage includes a metaphor?

    F "He looked out now at the school pool."

    G "He did see his parents sitting in the bleachers."

    H "He was a lion—strong, certain, powerful."

    J "It was almost time."

6 Read this sentence from the story.

> **Out of the water, he looked kind of klutzy and uncertain of himself, but the pool loved him.**

This sentence includes an example of

    A personification

    B metaphor

    C symbolism

    D foreshadowing

7 For Elliot, the pool is **most likely** a symbol of

F summer

G his strength and ability

H new beginnings

J magic

8 Which of the following could foreshadow the story's end?

A "His teammate Morales brought over the heat sheet, and Elliot looked it over."

B "It was almost time."

C "Elliott was the captain of the swim team, and he was most certainly ready—for a big win."

D "This was why Elliott had always loved swimming."

CHAPTER 11

Writing and Responding to Literature

Lesson 40: Writing Poems

In this lesson, you are going to practice writing your own poetry. Poetry was discussed in Chapter 8; if you would find it helpful, go back to Lesson 27 in that chapter, and review before you get started.

Remember, poems have the following characteristics:

- organized into stanzas (groups of lines)
- use rhythm (a structured pattern of sounds, alternating between weak and strong or sound and silence, creating a beat)
- may include rhyme (when words end with the same sound)
- use imagery (words that make pictures in your mind)

Choose your Style

To write your poem, choose one of the forms we discussed in Chapter 8. Possibilities include haiku, limerick, ballad, lyric, sonnet, and ode. Each form is described in detail in Lesson 27.

Be Creative

Use imagery and rhyme if you are inspired to do so. Most important, use words that you are comfortable with.

Choose a Topic

You can write a poem about absolutely anything, from a car to a dog to a sport to a flower. A list of sample topics is below; feel free to use one of these or to make up your own topic. Find one that appeals to you.

Sample Topics

- A dream you had
- Something in nature: for example, the ocean, a tree, a flower, the weather
- Animals: for example, dogs, cats, horses, zebras, your pet
- A friend or family member
- Your favorites: food, book, activity, sport

Then, use a separate sheet of paper to draft your poem. Be creative!

Use the lines below to freewrite or brainstorm on your topic.

Lesson 41
Answering Short-Response Questions

During your school years, you will often have to respond to questions by writing out an answer. These are called open-ended or short-response questions. Sometimes you will have to write only a short paragraph. Other times you will have to write a much longer response. On the New York State test, you will have to answer some short-response questions in response to passages you read. This lesson will help you write more effective responses.

Remember that a well-written short-response answer will:

1. **Include a clearly stated main idea.** The main idea of your answer usually includes both the question and your answer. It is also the first sentence of your answer. For example:

   Question: Why do you like to play soccer?

   Answer: I like to play soccer because I love running and kicking the ball.

2. **Use complete sentences.** Always write in complete sentences when you answer a short response question. Your answer should not be just one word or a couple of words.

3. **Use supporting details.** Use details from the story to support your answer. Details are things you learned in the story. They may be about any of the story's elements, such as the setting, a character, the plot, etc. Using details shows that you have read and understood the story. You don't need to use all of the details from the story, just those that help support your answer.

4. **Complete your answer with a simple conclusion.** At the end of your response, restate the main idea or thesis from your first sentence. In a longer response, you may summarize your main points.

Read this story and then review the sample answers to the short-response question that follows.

Felice on the Farm

by Rosemary Lee

When she was 8, Felice went to spend the summer on her grandparents' farm. She had visited the farm only once before, and, growing up in the city, had no experience with animals. Felice was small for her age, and pale from many months spent inside her apartment. She was glad to see her grandmother at the train station, but was also nervous about the summer ahead of her. What would she do on a farm? Her grandma took her suitcase and settled her in the car, and off they went. Felice was silent the whole way there.

The next day, Grandpa came and woke Felice up when it was still dark outside. She moaned and rolled over. Grandpa turned on the light in her room. "Felice, come on, honey. You're helping me with the cows," said Grandpa. Then he turned and went back downstairs.

Felice sat up. With the cows? What could he mean? She had never touched a cow in her life. She got up and got dressed and met her grandpa in the kitchen. Silently, she followed him out to the barn, and once inside the barn, he sat her on a stool and showed her how to milk a cow. At first she didn't want to touch the cow's udder, but when she did, it wasn't so bad. Pretty soon, Felice was milking a cow!

Soon Felice had a routine on the farm. She got up early every morning to help Grandpa with the cows, and then she helped her grandmother in the garden, where they grew corn, tomatoes, eggplant, beans, and lots of flowers, which Grandma said were her "special treat to herself, just for show." Felice would help her grandma cook in the afternoon sometimes, and if she weren't needed, she would roam the farm, running through fields and woods that seemed to stretch forever. At the end of the summer, Felice looked like a different child. She felt like one, too. She had grown taller and stronger and had learned so much. She even smiled more often and was no longer silent so much of the time. Part of her wanted to stay on the farm forever. She missed her mother and sister, though. She asked her grandma if she could come back next year, and her grandma said she would have to; they didn't know how they would get along without her now.

The day before she went home on the train, Felice by herself baked a blueberry pie to take home. She knew it turned out well and was proud of her work. She helped her grandpa with the cows one last time, and then she hugged Liza, her favorite cow. She hugged Grandpa, too, and went to the car where Grandma was waiting. Her suitcase and her pie were all packed. She took a deep breath and looked around. She had become a farm girl over the summer.

Jamar, Martine, and Kavi all read this story and then answered the following short-response question—

How does Felice change over the summer?

Let's take a look at each answer and then evaluate it, to see how complete it is. Each answer also includes a score. A score of 0 is the lowest score and a score of 2 is the highest score. The English Language Arts test that you will take uses this same scoring system. Below the sample answers you'll see something called a "Scoring Rubric." This explains what a 2-point answer looks like, what a 1-point answer looks like, and what a 0-point answer looks like.

Sample Answer 1: Jamar's Answer
Score: 0 points

During her summer at the farm, Felice changes a little.

Why does Jamar's answer score 0 points?

Jamar's answer is incomplete. It does not include any supporting details from the passage.

Sample Answer 2: Martine's Answer
Score: 1 point

Felice changes a lot over the summer. She learns to milk a cow and to grow crops. She changes on the farm.

Why does Martine's answer score 1 point?

Martine's answer includes a main idea: she has also restated the question to create her thesis statement. Martine uses complete sentences. However, she does not use enough supporting details from the story in her response. She needs to develop her answer more fully.

287287287287

287287

287

Sample Answer 3: Kavi's Answer
Score: 2 points

> Over the summer she spends at the farm, Felice changes a lot. She learns to do many things, such as milk a cow and bake a pie and work in a garden. This is all new to her, because she is a city kid. Felice also changes in appearance. At the end of the summer she looks healthier and stronger. She changes inside, too. She is proud of herself, and she smiles more than she used to. Felice learns lots of important skills on the farm, but most important, she learns what she can do.

Why does Kavi's answer score 2 points?

Kavi's answer includes a main idea and uses complete sentences. He also uses many details from the story, including:

- Felice learns to milk a cow, bake a pie, and work in a garden.
- Felice looks healthier and stronger at the end of the summer.
- Felice feels more confident and smiles more at the end of the summer.

Finally, Kavi closes his answer with a concluding sentence.

Below is the Scoring Rubric used to grade these sample responses. This rubric is similar to the one that will be used by New York State to grade your English Language Arts test.

Score	To get this score, you—
2	Answered the question fully and used at least three details that explain how Felice has changed over the summer. You included details such as what Felice learned to do (milk a cow, bake a pie, work in a garden) and other ways in which she is changed (physically and inside) during her summer on the farm. The response was focused and clear.
1	Included some correct information, but the response was too general. You did not give enough details to support his or her answer.
0	Wrote a response that was unclear, had incorrect information, or did not respond to the question.

Now it's your turn. Read the story below, and then answer the short response question that follows. As you plan your answer, remember the following keys to a successful short-response answer:

1. **Include a clearly stated main idea.**
2. **Use complete sentences.**
3. **Use supporting details. Remember: you don't need to use all of the details from the story; just those that help support your answer.**
4. **Complete your answer with a simple concluding sentence.**

The New Addition

by Joe Meneer

Carlos had been looking forward to the arrival of his little brother or sister for months, but now that the time for the baby to be born was almost here, he was having second thoughts. He knew that his parents were still excited about the baby, but Carlos had begun to see all the possibilities for disaster with a baby around. What if the baby got into his toys or his art supplies? What if it tore up his books or messed up his room? Carlos tried not to think about it, because the baby was coming soon, and there was no sending it back.

Within a week, the baby was born, and Carlos took on the important role of big brother. He had a baby sister now. Her name was Angela. Carlos was excited about the baby. Maybe everything would be all right.

Then Carlos's dad told him that his mother really needed his help, because she was going to need some time to get her strength back after the delivery.

So Carlos might need to help them out, and also take care of himself a little more than usual while the baby got used to the house. They were counting on him, said his father, to help show Angela how things worked in their house.

It turned out there was nothing you could show Angela. Brand new babies couldn't do anything, it seemed, except nurse and cry and dirty up diaper after diaper. Carlos couldn't imagine that he had ever been such a needy child. For a few days he was as helpful as he could be. He got his own breakfast, he was quiet when the baby was asleep, he helped his dad make all the meals.

After a few days, though, Carlos was bored with being the responsible big brother. As far as he could tell, Angela had no use for him at all. He wasn't even sure his parents remembered that Angela had a big brother. All they talked about was the baby, and they took loads of pictures of her to e-mail people. Friends and neighbors kept coming by with presents and food, all in honor of Angela, who just lay there like a lump, unless she was screaming her head off, which was pretty often, it seemed.

Carlos was tired of hearing about Angela. He didn't even want to see her. What he wanted was for things to go back to normal, when they all spent time together, and his dad played catch with him, and they would have a family video night. Angela didn't watch any TV.

One afternoon Carlos's mother asked him to watch the baby for a moment. Angela wasn't asleep. She was just lying there on the bed, looking around with her big eyes. She made a face like she might cry, and Carlos reached over and touched her hand with his finger. Quickly, Angela grabbed his finger. He leaned over her, and

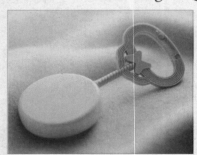

she stared at him, keeping a tight grip on his finger. When his mom came back in, Carlos was still in the same position. "She really likes me, Mom. She won't let go of my finger," said Carlos, glowing.

"Of course she likes you, Carlos. You're her big brother. You'll be her favorite person in the world." Carlos smiled.

Now answer the following question on your own paper.

Explain how Carlos feels about his new baby sister. How do his feelings for her change in the course of the story?

Writing Practice

Read this story. Using your own paper, answer the short-response question that follows.

The Treasure

by Eileen Grayson

On his way home from school, Ray found a wallet. He brought it home and looked inside. There was no license or anything, but there was $25 in the back compartment. Ray knew that he should turn the money in to someone, but he wanted to enjoy having found it first. He imagined what he might do with $25, and how many baseball cards he could buy with that much money. It was so exciting, really. Before he got carried away, he closed the wallet up and took it down to the office, where his dad was working.

"Hey, Dad," he said.

"Hi, Ray. Come on in. What can I do for you?"

"Well, I found this on the way home from school today," said Ray sheepishly. He knew he should have brought the wallet to his dad right away.

His dad thought they should put up "Found" posters, and he and Ray spent a few hours making one up and getting it copied and then sticking them up on telephone poles and lampposts around the area where Ray found the wallet. They had a call the next afternoon from a man who described the wallet accurately, right down to the $25. He had lost it while doing landscaping at the Emersons' house. He stopped by and picked up his wallet that evening, and thanked Ray for being honest about it. Before he left, he shook Ray's hand, and then he opened the wallet and took out the $5 bill, and handed it to Ray as a reward. A reward! Ray couldn't believe it.

Answer this question. Review the Editing Checklist before completing your response, and make any necessary corrections.

1 **What is the theme of this passage? Use details from the text to support your answer.**

_____

_____

_____

_____

_____

_____

_____

_____

_____

_____

Editing Checklist

1 Check your capitalization and punctuation.

2 Spell all words correctly.

3 Check for sentence fragments or run-on sentences.

4 Keep verb tense consistent.

5 Make sure subjects and verbs agree.

6 Use words according to the rules of Standard English.

7 Remember to paragraph correctly.

UNIT

III Mechanics

GETTING THE IDEA

In this final unit, you will review some of the "mechanics" of writing. That's the nuts and bolts of using language correctly, beginning with writing effective sentences. Because nearly everything you write will have the sentence as its foundation, Chapter 12 is all about writing effective sentences. You will be able to recognize and correct a sentence fragment, understand simple and complex sentences, and use different types and lengths of sentences to create interesting and effective writing.

Finally, we'll review some grammar and punctuation rules and practice with lots of examples. The information you review in this unit will help you write more concise and effective answers to the open-ended questions on the ELA test. That's the purpose of this book, after all.

In the following two chapters, this Unit will help you:

- identify and understand sentence structure
- avoid and correct sentence fragments
- make your writing interesting by varying the length of your sentences
- use the comma correctly
- know when to capitalize words
- learn spelling patterns
- understand subject-verb agreement
- edit your writing for punctuation and grammar

By the end of this Unit, you will understand how correct punctuation and grammar can make your writing more effective. Let's get started!

Performance Indicators: W.CPI.7, W.CPI.8

CHAPTER 12

Writing Effective Sentences

Lesson 42: Simple and Compound Sentences

The sentence is the building block of writing. Almost everything you write will be made up of sentences of different types and lengths. The most interesting writing uses a combination of different types of sentences to keep the reader's attention.

Simple Sentences

Sentences are made up of clauses: A **clause** is a group of words with a subject and a predicate that expresses a thought. A **simple sentence** is made up of one **independent clause** (a clause that can stand on its own as a sentence; also called a main clause). It expresses just one thought and has just one subject and just one predicate. The **subject** of the sentence is who or what the sentence is about: *Mary, I, the dog, you*—these could all be subjects. The **predicate** is the part of the sentence that contains the verb. It is the part of the sentence that describes something the subject is or does: *sees a movie, runs on the beach, eats a sandwich*—these could all be predicates. Below is a simple sentence.

Helen walked to school.

Here is another simple sentence. This one is longer and includes modifiers.

Joachim and Helen walked to school and sang songs.

This is still a simple sentence because it contains only one independent clause. The subject is *Joachim and Helen* and the predicate is *walked to school and sang songs*.

A subject doesn't have to be a concrete thing or a physical object. It can be an idea. For example, in the sentence "Time passed by" the subject is *time*.

Compound Sentences

A **compound sentence** is two (or more) simple sentences put together. It has two (or more) independent clauses: two (or more) subjects, predicates, and ideas. These clauses should be related and are often joined by a semicolon (;) or a **coordinating conjunction** (such as *and, or, yet,* or *but*).

> Ray likes to dance, but Heather prefers swimming.

In this sentence, the two clauses are "Ray likes to dance" and "Heather prefers swimming." They are joined by a comma and the conjunction *but.* There are two subjects in this compound sentence, *Ray* and *Heather,* and two verbs, *likes* and *prefers.* The parts of the sentence are related: both describe activities that the subjects enjoy.

Coordinating Conjunctions	
and	so
but	or
for	yet

 Read the sentence below, then answer the question in a complete sentence.

> Ayla and Lucas went to the movies.

What kind of sentence is this?

_____

_____

_____

 Does the sentence have one or two main clauses?

Example 1

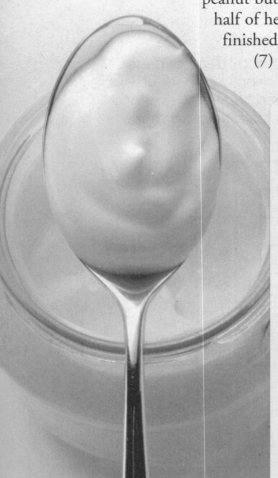

(1) Jamar and Yoshe ate lunch. (2) Jamar had soup; Yoshe had a peanut butter sandwich. (3) Yoshe wasn't very hungry. (4) She ate half of her sandwich, and Jamar ate the other half. (5) Then Jamar finished his own lunch. (6) He ate pretzels, grapes, and a yogurt. (7) Jamar finished lunch, and then he had a snack.

1a **Which sentence from the passage is a simple sentence?**

A   1

B   2

C   4

D   7

Which choice has only one main clause?

1b **Which sentence from the passage is a compound sentence?**

F   1

G   3

H   4

J   6

Discuss your answer with your teacher or class.

Lesson 43
Sentence Fragments

A complete sentence will include a subject and a predicate. If a sentence is missing one of these elements, it is called a **sentence fragment**. Sentence fragments do not express a complete thought, and therefore do not make sense on their own. Fragments are sometimes used purposely in poetry and in speech (and in dialogue), but they are otherwise incorrect in writing. Usually a sentence fragment can be corrected by adding either a subject or a predicate.

> Went to the pool.

This sentence is missing its *subject*. By adding a subject, the sentence makes sense and is no longer a fragment.

> <u>Yoshe and Martine</u> went to the pool.

Below is another fragment. This one is missing its *predicate*.

> Ella's love for art.

This fragment is corrected with the addition of a predicate, which includes the verb or the action of the sentence.

> Ella's love for art <u>was obvious to her teachers</u>.

A sentence fragment may also consist of a **dependent clause**. This type of fragment usually has both its subject and verb, but it is not a complete sentence because the clause begins with a word such as *after, because, if, since* or *unless*. A dependent clause requires an independent clause to be a complete sentence.

> Unless you read the book.

This is a sentence fragment. Below is how you could correct it.

> Unless you read the book, you won't know how the story ends.

Phrases and words that are missing both a subject and a verb are also sentence fragments. Often such fragments can be corrected by combining them with another sentence in a passage.

> Sara and her family went on vacation. To Florida.

"To Florida" is a fragment. It is related to the sentence right before it. The two sentences can be combined, eliminating the fragment.

> Sarah and her family went on vacation to Florida.

Combining Sentences

You can also combine a fragment with a complete sentence by replacing the period in the complete sentence with a comma; adding a joining word such as *and, but, however, including,* or *so*; and then adding the fragment. Here is an example:

> There are many kinds of trees in this area. Elms, oaks, spruce, and pine.

"Elms, oaks, spruce, and pine" is a sentence fragment. Notice that it has no verb. To correct it, combine the full sentence with the fragment.

> There are many kinds of trees in this area, including elms, oaks, spruce, and pine.

Here's another example.

> Lara is sick. Stayed home from school.

This can be fixed to read:

> Lara is sick, so she stayed home from school.

Use your best judgment when combining sentences, and be sure that the new sentence has the same essential meaning as the originals.

Example 1

1 **Which of the following is NOT a complete sentence?**

   A   Omar put the groceries away.

   B   Jenny loves chocolate.

   C   They have six kids.

   D   Went to the store.

Which sentence does not have a subject and predicate?

Example 2

2 **Choose the BEST way to combine the following sentence and sentence fragment.**

The stew contained many types of vegetables. Not my favorite, corn.

   F   The stew contained many types of vegetables not my favorite, corn.

   G   The stew contained many types of vegetables, not my favorite, corn.

   H   The stew contained many types of vegetables, so not my favorite, corn.

   J   The stew contained many types of vegetables, but not my favorite, corn.

Discuss your answer with your teacher or class.

Lesson 44
Sentence Variety

Sometimes there are no sentence fragments, but there are several small sentences that read awkwardly. Or perhaps a passage has many lengthy sentences, which can become confusing to the reader. Just as it's a good idea to vary the words you use when writing, it's also a good idea to have **sentence variety**, which can help keep the reader interested.

Here is an example of a number of shorter sentences that read awkwardly.

> In the winter it is cold. We get snow rather than rain. I like to go sledding when it snows.

These sentences make sense, but they are choppy. Short, choppy sentences can be distracting. To make them read more smoothly, try combining some or all of them, using punctuation and conjunctions appropriately.

> I like to go sledding in the winter when it is cold and we get snow instead of rain.

You may also change, add, and eliminate words to fix an awkward passage. Another way of combining the three sentences is the following:

> During the winter it snows because it is cold, so I get to go sledding.

It's not necessary to eliminate all short sentences—sometimes a short sentence is a very effective way of conveying information. And a short sentence can break up too many long sentences. The point of sentence variety is not to have too many long sentences back-to-back or too many short ones.

THINKING IT THROUGH Read the passage below, then answer the question that follows.

> Jan likes chocolate. Chocolate tastes good. Hot chocolate is delicious.

How would you change these short sentences to make this passage read more smoothly?

_____

_____

_____

HINT! Can you combine a few of these short sentences?

You may also find that you have written a number of long and complicated sentences in one piece of writing. This can be confusing and tiring for the reader. To make the passage read better, you should break up some of these longer sentences. Do not break up all of them—this will leave your passage filled with short, choppy sentences. The idea behind varying your sentences is to create a balance.

Here is a passage with some long sentences that contain a lot of information and may confuse the reader.

> Jackie wanted to go to the movies on Saturday to see the Marx Brothers festival, because she really loved the Marx Brothers and enjoyed their style of humor. Unfortunately, Jackie couldn't go on Saturday because she had a previous engagement with her friend Roberta, who couldn't stand the Marx Brothers because she found their humor too silly.

Here is the passage rewritten to vary the sentence length.

> Jackie wanted to go to the movies on Saturday to see the Marx Brothers festival. She really loved the Marx Brothers and enjoyed their style of humor. Unfortunately, Jackie couldn't go on Saturday because she had a previous engagement with her friend Roberta. Roberta couldn't stand the Marx Brothers for she found their humor too silly.

There are many possible ways of rewriting this passage. When writing your own work, try to be aware of sentence length. Reading your writing aloud can help make you more aware.

Example 1

Kavi needed to go to the library to do research for his history paper on the Harlem Renaissance, a time during which African-Americans produced great music and art. The 1920s became an important period in Harlem, and hundreds of artists of all kinds traveled there in search of opportunity.

5 **Rewrite this short passage to break up the long sentences and make the passage easier to understand.**

_____

_____

_____

_____

_____

Be sure not to change the original meaning of the passage.

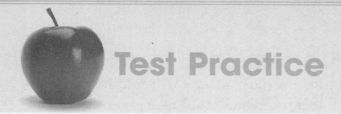

Test Practice

Read this article. Then answer questions 1 through 3.

(1) The George Eastman House is in Rochester. (2) Eastman helped change the movie business with his emulsion film, and motion picture film became his bestseller. (3) In 1900. (4) He presented his Brownie camera. (5) It sold for $1. (6) It revolutionized photography. (7) Suddenly anyone could take photos. (8) Eastman died in 1932. (9) He donated more than $100 million in his lifetime. (10) The bulk of his donations went to colleges and universities, including the University of Rochester, Massachusetts Institute of Technology, and Tuskegee Institute. (11) His home in Rochester was opened as the International Museum of Photography in 1947.

1 Which sentence in the article is a sentence fragment?

   A 1

   B 8

   C 3

   D 10

2 Which sentence in the article is a compound sentence?

   F 1

   G 2

   H 6

   J 9

3 Read the following sentences from the article.

(3) In 1900. (4) He presented his Brownie camera. (5) It sold for $1. (6) It revolutionized photography. (7) Suddenly anyone could take photos.

Rewrite these sentences to make the passage flow more smoothly.

_____

_____

_____

_____

_____

Read this story. Then answer questions 4 through 6.

Matilde was so tired of pizza. Yet, here they all were, out for pizza again. At least they weren't having takeout on the porch. They had eaten out or had takeout every night for the last two weeks, and this was just the beginning. They were having their kitchen redone, which was likely to take at least three months. Matilde couldn't imagine what they'd be eating by the end of this adventure. They were working their way through every restaurant in town. In another week, they'd only have the takeout option.

Mostly, this was because of the twins. Nate and Nora terrorized the wait staff and the other diners wherever they went. The twins were three years old, but seemed to be part of some primitive breed of mammal. They rarely seemed to consume anything. Mostly, they threw their food at each other. And at her. And at Donny and Grace. If you had five kids, there ought to be special restaurants for you. There probably were, but her parents were too busy or ill-informed to find them, not that it mattered; Matilde was pretty sure they'd wear out their welcome in the worst restaurant in the world inside of five minutes. How long would it take tonight?

4 Which of the following is a simple sentence from the story?

  A "The twins were three years old, but seemed to be part of some primitive breed of mammal."

  B "And at Donny and Grace."

  C "They had eaten out or had takeout every night for the last two weeks, and this was just the beginning."

  D "Matilde was so tired of pizza."

5 Which sentence from the story is a fragment?

  F "Mostly, this was because of the twins."

  G "They rarely seemed to consume anything."

  H "And at her."

  J "Mostly, they threw their food at each other."

6 Read the following sentence from the story.

There probably were, but her parents were too busy or ill-informed to find them, not that it mattered; Matilde was pretty sure they'd wear out their welcome in the worst restaurant in the world inside of five minutes.

Rewrite the sentence in the space below to make it easier to understand.

_____

_____

_____

_____

Performance Indicator: W.CPI.7

CHAPTER
13

Grammar and Editing Skills

Lesson 45: The Comma

A **comma** (,) is a punctuation that is used to indicate a transition or separation in a sentence. Commas are most often used

- before a conjunction when linking two different ideas or phrases
- after introductory words or phrases
- to separate items in a series
- to set off a direct quotation
- between the day and year in a date

When linking ideas or phrases with a conjunction (such as *and, or,* or *but*), you should put the comma <u>before</u> the conjunction.

Herman went to the laboratory, and then he went back home.

We could go to a movie, or we could go see a play.

You can rent a car if you want to, but it will be cheaper to take the subway.

Commas are also used after introductory words in a sentence.

After the movie, we all went out for ice cream.

Although we try hard, our team doesn't win many games.

Before you go to school today, be sure to put your lunch in your backpack.

Unless we fix our computer, we won't be able to do the project.

When you are listing several items in a series, commas are used after each item, but <u>not</u> after the last item on the list.

> Cindy plays soccer, basketball, and baseball.

> Erin likes polka music, disco, and waltzes.

> John, Steve, Wilma, and Bea are going to come with us.

Use a comma before a direct quotation and between the day and year in a date.

> Janet replied, "You're not my sister."

> July 4, 1776

Use a comma between the names of a city, town, or state and the larger region it is found in. Use a comma after the larger region if the sentence continues.

> Nydia lives in Albany, New York.

> Nydia visits Paris, France, every five years.

Example 1

---

1   **Choose the sentence that has correct punctuation.**

A   I like candy, cake, and peanut, butter.

B   Fran would go to the store, but she would rather stay home.

C   Unfortunately Bert, is not here.

D   Let's all play a game or, we can watch a movie.

Which choice has a conjunction?

Example 2

2 **Where should commas be added in this sentence?**

I usually eat pancakes for breakfast but sometimes I like waffles.

F I usually eat pancakes, for breakfast but sometimes, I like waffles.

G I usually eat pancakes for, breakfast, but sometimes I like waffles.

H I usually eat pancakes for breakfast, but sometimes I like waffles.

J I usually eat pancakes for breakfast but, sometimes I like waffles.

Remember that a comma goes after introductory words and before a conjunction.

Example 3

3 **Which of the following has a comma in the wrong place?**

A When Charlie gets here, we can go out to eat.

B I like soup, chicken, and rice.

C He wanted to take a nap but, he didn't have time.

D JoAnne asked, "Do you have a scarf I can borrow?"

Discuss your answer with your teacher or class.

Lesson 46
Capitalization

Capital letters, or uppercase letters, are used only in certain situations. Capital letters tell us something about words. They are mostly used at the beginning of

- words that begin a sentence
- proper names (including people's names and nicknames; geographical names; and the names of languages, organizations, days, months, holidays, historical periods and events, historical documents, and religions)
- abbreviations and acronyms (in this case, all letters are usually capitalized—for example, FBI, YMCA, or NAACP
- personal titles before a person's name (Dr., Mr., Mrs.)
- the first and last word in a title, and other important words in a title (*The Wind in the Willow*)
- the pronoun *I* (referring to oneself)

If you see a capitalized word, you know that it likely falls into one of these categories.

 Read the passsage below, then answer the question that follows.

mr. Johnson runs the bookstore downtown. i just bought the railway children from him last week.

Rewrite this sentence with the correct capitalization.

_____

_____

_____

 Are there any proper nouns in the sentence? Titles?

Example 1

1 **Which choice correctly capitalizes this sentence?**

> *everybody knows that mr. evans works for greenpeace.*

A Everybody knows that Mr. Evans works for greenpeace.

B Everybody knows that Mr. Evans works for Greenpeace.

C Everybody knows that Mr. evans works for greenpeace.

D Everybody knows that Mr. Evans Works for greenpeace.

Review the list of items that should be capitalized.

Example 2

2 **What is the proper way to capitalize the title of this book?**

> *I have written a book entitled the birds and the big bad wolf.*

F The birds and the big bad Wolf

G The Birds And The Big Bad Wolf

H The Birds and The Big Bad Wolf

J The Birds and the Big Bad Wolf

Discuss your answer with your teacher or class.

Lesson 47
Spelling

For some, spelling in English can be really frustrating. Different letters can make the same sound—as in *here* and *hear*. The same letters can make different sounds—as with *ou* in *bought*, *bounce*, and *tour*. There are no hard and fast rules, and it can definitely be confusing.

Still, you need to be able to spell correctly. Mostly, we learn to spell by practicing—by reading and writing and memorizing lists of spelling words. There are, however, some general rules and hints you can

Spelling Rules

- To determine whether to use *ie* or *ei*: remember words with a long *e* (rhymes with *me*) are spelled *ie*, and words that have a sound other than a long *e* generally are spelled *ei*.

  Example: *Relieve* has a long *e* sound, and *weight* has a long *a* sound. (One notable exception: *weird*. No *c* and no *a* sound, just remember it's weird.)

- When adding a suffix beginning with a vowel to a word ending with an unpronounced –e, drop the e.

  Example: The noun form of *behave* would be *behavior*.

- When adding a suffix beginning with a consonant to a word ending with an unpronounced –e, retain the e.

  Example: The adverb form of *divine* would be *divinely*.

- When pluralizing nouns ending in -s, -z, -x, -sh, or -ch, add –es.

  Example: The plural of *gas* is *gases*.

Spelling Rules (continued)

- When pluralizing nouns ending in –y, drop the *y* and add –ies.

  Example: The plural of *body* is *bodies*.

- When pluralizing nouns that end with –f, change the *f* to *v* and add –es.

  Example: The plural of *leaf* is *leaves*.

- When a one-syllable word ends in a consonant after one vowel, double the final consonant before adding a suffix that begins with a vowel.

  Example: *bat* becomes *batting, batted, batter*.

- If the word has more than one syllable, but the accent or emphasis is on the final syllable, the same rule applies: double the final consonant.

  Examples: *control—controlled, controlling*; *prefer—preferring, preferred*

Example 1

Imelda found it unbeleiveable that there were no tickets left for the consert. She wanted to go sew badly, she was upset for daze.

1 **Rewrite this sentence in the space below, correcting the spelling error(s).**

_____

_____

_____

 Discuss your answer with your teacher or class.

Lesson 48
Subject-Verb Agreement

In Chapter 12, we talked about subjects and verbs in clauses. In this lesson, we are focusing on subject-verb agreement. **Subject-verb agreement** simply means using the right verb for the subject. A singular subject takes a singular verb, and a plural subject takes a plural verb. Usually, you assign the correct nouns and verbs automatically, because you know what sounds right and what doesn't.

Singular   Jim <u>goes</u> to the store.

Plural   Jim and his mom <u>go</u> to the store.

Verb agreement can get tricky when you're not sure whether the subject is singular or plural. Once you know that, it's easy to select the correct verb. Below is a chart with a few rules to help you avoid confusion.

Verb Rules

- Don't be confused by words that appear between the subject and the verb. The sentence below is correct.

  Example: The <u>table</u> under the trees <u>is</u> covered with a tablecloth.

- Indefinite pronouns such as "each," "everyone," "everybody," "anybody," "anyone," "none," "nobody," "neither," "somebody," and "someone" are singular; other indefinite pronouns are plural: "both," "few," "many," "several."

  Example: <u>Everyone</u> <u>eats</u> at the Indian restaurant.
  Example: Several <u>cans</u> of paint <u>spill</u> onto the floor.

- Subjects joined by "and," such as "Jim and his mom," "orange and green" and "pen, notebook, and book," are plural.

  Example: <u>Rice and chicken</u> <u>are</u> the main ingredients.

Verb Rules (continued)

- Subjects joined by "and" and acting as a unit should be treated as singular, and take a singular verb.

   Example: <u>Beans and rice is</u> my favorite food.

- Subjects joined by "nor" and "or" take the form of the subject closest to the verb.

   Example: Neither my jacket nor <u>my boots are</u> in the hallway.
   Either the games or <u>the doll is</u> on the table.

- Plural words that have singular meanings, such as "20 dollars," "two-thirds," and "37 pounds," take singular verbs.

   Example: <u>Twenty dollars is</u> a huge tip.

- Even if a title of a work sounds plural, like *The Grapes of Wrath* does, it's always singular.

   Example: Elvis Presley's <u>*Greatest Hits* is</u> worth buying.

Just remember: when working with agreement, first find the subject. Then ask yourself if it's singular or plural. After that, it should be easy to pick the right verb for the job.

Example 1

> **1** **Which sentence is written correctly?**
>
> **A** Doris want a new car.
>
> **B** The box of tissues is on the table.
>
> **C** I are really in a good mood.
>
> **D** The boys in the garage was working on an invention.

Remember to first find the subject and determine whether it's singular or plural.

Lesson 49
Editing Task

In this chapter, you learned how to use grammar correctly. You also practiced how to correct grammar errors in sentences. On the New York State test, you will be asked to edit a paragraph. This means that you will have to fix the errors. The paragraph will have mistakes in capital letters and punctuation.

- Do you remember which words always begin with a capital letter?
- Do you remember when to use a comma?

These are the kinds of mistakes you will find in the paragraph. On the test, you will have a chance to practice with your teacher. You will see two paragraphs. The first one is called the Practice Task. With your teacher, you will find and correct the errors in this paragraph. Your teacher will make sure that you understand what to do. Then you will fix the mistakes in the second paragraph. This is called the Editing Task. Only the Editing Task is graded.

The editing task is scored like this:	
3 points	No more than one error, either new or not corrected, remains after you have corrected the paragraph.
2 points	Two to three errors, either new or not corrected, remain after you have corrected the paragraph.
1 point	Four to five errors, either new or not corrected, remain after you have corrected the paragraph.
0 points	Six or more errors, either new or not corrected, remain after you have corrected the paragraph.

Ready to practice? Complete the tasks on the next page.

Sample
There are some mistakes in this paragraph. Let's correct them together.

When I grow up, I want to be a Baker. I already knows how to bake many things. My Aunt has taught me how to bake cookies bread, and even cakes. We bake together. Every Saturday. One day, I'm going to opened up my own bakery.

Editing Task
Here is a report a student wrote. There are some mistakes in the paragraph. Some sentences may have more than one mistake, and other sentences may contain no mistakes at all. There are <u>no</u> mistakes in spelling.

Read the paragraph and find the mistakes. Draw a line through each mistake in the paragraph. Then write the correction above it.

My visit to the planetarium last week was a lot of fun. A guide takes us to the different rooms and explained the exhibits to us. She told us about the Planets in our solar system. We learned that jupiter is the most largest planet. We also learned that the Earth is made up mostly of water. The guide also showed us some of the equipment that astronauts uses to survive in space.

Test Practice

Read this article. Then answer questions 1 through 4.

(1) Aaron Copland was born in brooklyn, New York, On November 14 1900. (2) He new by age 16 that he wanted to be a composer. (3) In 1921 he went to Paris and studied with nadia boulanger. (4) When he returned to New York in 1924, he had his first job, writing an organ piece for Madame Boulanger. (5) In New York in the 1920s Copland was influenced by jazz music in Harlem. (6) In the 1930s, he made a change in his style. (7) He began to write simpler music and created a number of well-known works based on American folk tales. (8) The best known of these are *Billy the Kid* and *Rodeo*. (9) He won a Pulitzer Prize in Music in 1945 for *Appalachian Spring*, a ballet he composed for Martha Graham, and an Academy Award for Best Original Score in 1950 for the movie *the heiress*. (10) Copland stopped composing in 1970, though he continued to lecture and conduct for 15 years more. (11) He died in Tarrytown in 1990. (12) Many music critics considers him one of the great composers.

NOTICE: Photocopying any part of this book is forbidden by law.

317

1   Which sentence in the article has a spelling error?

     A   1

     B   2

     C   8

     D   11

2   Which sentence in the article has a capitalization error?

     F   3

     G   6

     H   7

     J   11

3   Read the following sentence from the article.

     Aaron Copland was born in brooklyn, New York, on November 14 1900.

     Rewrite this sentence in the space below, correcting any errors.

_____

_____

_____

_____

4   Which sentence from the article contains an error in subject-verb agreement?

     A   2

     B   4

     C   9

     D   12

Read this story. Then answer questions 5 through 8.

(1) Shemar is trying to earn money so he can attend baseball camp next summer. (2) He delivers newspapers on weekdays and cut grass on weekends. (3) He also babysits and tutors a younger kid in math most weekends. (4) All in all, Shemar is very bizzy. (5) sometimes he can't even remember what day it is. (6) He also have to keep up with his homework. (7) If his grades fall even a small bit, his parents will make him give up at least one job, and then, no baseball camp. (8) Shemar is determined that he will go to baseball camp. (9) After three months, his hard work is finally paying off. (10) He saved $75 by Thanksgiving. (11) The deposit for camp is due January 1. (12) Though he didn't due much yard work in the winter he still had newspaper delivery babysitting and tutoring. (13) He would certainly have the deposit on time.

NOTICE: Photocopying any part of this book is forbidden by law.

319

5 Which sentence from the story includes a subject-verb agreement error?

   F   1

   G   5

   H   6

   J   9

6 Which sentence from the story has a spelling error?

   A   2

   B   6

   C   7

   D   13

7 Read the following sentence from the story.

> **Though he didn't due much yard work in the winter he still had newspaper delivery babysitting and tutoring.**

Rewrite the sentence in the space below, correcting any errors.

_____

_____

_____

8 Which sentence from the story contains a capitalization error?

   F   5

   G   7

   H   10

   J   11

POSTTEST

English Language Arts

BOOK 1

Book 1

Reading

*D*irections

In this part of the test, you will do some reading. Then you will answer questions about what you have read. For the multiple-choice questions, you will mark your answers on the answer sheet. For question 21, you will write your answer directly in the book.

Read this story. Then answer questions 1 through 5.

How do animals who neither hibernate nor migrate survive the harsh Northeastern winter? Ned Warden is a biologist at the State University of New York at Plattsburgh. In this interview, he discusses ways certain animals store food for the winter.

Interviewer:	Everyone knows that bears hibernate through the winter and that this allows them to survive without eating for long months. But how do other animals manage to survive?
Ned:	Yes, it's true that bears do hibernate during the cold months. Their bodies live off the fat they have stored from eating in the fall. A few other animals actually hide supplies of food during the fall, which they then eat during the winter.
Interviewer:	Kind of like the story of the Ant and the Grasshopper?
Ned:	[*laughing*] Yes, exactly.
Interviewer:	So which other animals store their food? I know squirrels hide nuts throughout the fall.

Ned: You're right; squirrels are the animals everyone thinks of when they think of animals storing their food. They gather pinecones and various nuts, like acorns, and tuck them away in various hiding places. Beavers also do this as well. Although instead of storing nuts, they submerge branches underwater where they'll be preserved throughout the winter. Many birds, like the nuthatches and chickadees you may see at your bird feeder, also hide large quantities of seeds.

Interviewer: What about mice? I've sometimes come across tiny piles of dog food in my basement that I know my dog didn't put there.

Ned: Yes, mice that spend the winters inside warm homes and buildings definitely steal and hide food. Mice not lucky enough to live indoors also hide food in underground burrows.

Interviewer: It doesn't sound like that many animals store their food. Why is that?

Ned: There are many reasons. Food can spoil, even in the cold winter since the temperatures rise and fall constantly. Meat-eating animals would lose most of their stored food to spoilage—or to other animals that smelled the meat and got there first. However, a few animals will store meat for very short periods of time. Naturalist Bernd Heinrich found this to be true of ravens.

Interviewer: What happens if an animal eats all of the food it has stored?

Ned: Then it's time for the animal to scavenge for whatever it can find outdoors. Bernd Heinrich has actually discovered a really interesting thing about red squirrels. Apparently, they use their sharp teeth to make marks in the bark of sugar maple trees. This causes the sap stored in the tree to flow. The water in the sap eventually evaporates, leaving behind maple sugar. The red squirrels then hurry back to their trees and lick off the sugar. The energy in the sugar keeps them going when their nut supply is gone.

Interviewer: Wow—that's a lot like what people do to get sap out of trees and make maple sugar.

Ned: Yes. In his book *Winter World: The Ingenuity of Animal Survival*, Heinrich discusses how people may have actually learned this trick from squirrels. An old Iroquois myth tells the story of a boy who watches a squirrel licking the sap off a maple tree—and tries some, too.

Go On

1 Why are bears **not** likely to store food for winter use?

A Bears store the energy they need in their body fat.

B Bears cannot find hiding places large enough for all the food they need.

C Bears live off the food stored by other animals.

D Bears eat the sap off of maple trees.

2 Read this quote from the interview.

Then it's time for the animal to scavenge for whatever it can find outdoors.

What does "scavenge" mean?

F run

G search

H hide

J store

3 The Iroquois myth about the red squirrel shows us that

A Native Americans know how to talk to animals

B all animals know how to make maple sugar

C people may learn things from animals

D Bernd Heinrich thinks this story is amusing

4 According to Ned Warden, it doesn't make sense for most animals to store food during the winter because

F it takes too much work

G they have no good places to store food

H food may spoil or be stolen by other animals

J most animals don't know how to store food

5 The interviewer compares animals that store food for winter to the story of the Ant and the Grasshopper because

A he knows ants also store food for winter

B real animal behavior reminds him of this fable

C real ants and grasshoppers are a lot like the ones in this fable

D he thinks bears are a lot like grasshoppers

Book 1

Directions

Read this poem by Robert Louis Stevenson. Then answer questions 6 through 10.

A Visit from the Sea

By Robert Louis Stevenson

Far from the loud sea beaches
Where he goes fishing and crying,
Here in the inland garden
Why is the seagull flying?

Here are no fish to dive for;
Here is the corn and lea;
Here are the green trees rustling.
Hie away home to sea!

lea = field or pasture

hie = hurry

Fresh is the river water
And quiet among the rushes;
This is no home for the seagull
But for the rooks and thrushes.

rooks and thrushes are types of birds

Pity the bird that has wandered!
Pity the sailor ashore!
Hurry him home to the ocean,
Let him come here no more!

High on the sea cliff ledges
The white gulls are trooping and crying,
Here among the rooks and roses,
Why is the seagull flying?

Go On 325

6 What does the speaker of the poem tell us about the seagull?

F It has wandered far away from the ocean.

G It is flying above the ocean when he sees it.

H It flies better than rooks and thrushes.

J It was born near the river.

7 The poet uses the lines *High on the sea cliff ledges/ The white gulls are trooping and crying* to

A teach us a lesson about nature

B show us how beautiful the sea is

C describe the seagull's true home near the ocean

D explain how the seagull flew inland

8 Which statement best describes why this passage is a poem?

F It is about a real event that happened in ancient history.

G It was written to persuade the reader to believe in something.

H It is split into stanzas and has lines that rhyme.

J It was written to be performed on stage by actors.

9 Which of the following **best** describes the speaker in this poem?

A He is a sensitive person who cares about animals.

B He is a cruel person who dislikes birds.

C He never pays any attention to the natural world.

D He hopes to live near the ocean some day.

10 The poet compares the seagull to the sailor to show that

F the sailor is more at home on the ocean than the seagull

G the seagull is better adapted to life on the sea

H both the sailor and the seagull belong at sea

J sailors love seagulls

Book 1

Directions
Read this article. Then answer questions 11 through 15.

WINNING THE RIGHT TO VOTE

by Elmira Blake

Unbelievably, American women have had the right to vote for less than one hundred years! African-American women (and men) in some parts of the country have enjoyed this right for even less time. It took the hard work and conviction that all people deserve an equal voice to change the U.S. Constitution and grant women suffrage, or the right to vote.

It's not surprising that women also had few legal rights. A woman who divorced her husband immediately lost all rights to her children. Women couldn't vote, run for office, or serve on juries. In 1787, four million people lived in the U.S. Of this number, the Constitution granted only 160,000, or 4%, the right to vote. To vote, you had to be a white male property owner who was older than 21.

Background History

While the United States claimed independence in 1776, girls and women then did not share such freedom. Young girls quickly learned that their destinies would be to raise a family. Women couldn't own property, such as homes or land. They also had no right to their own money, even if they earned it themselves. Many African-American women lived as slaves. In addition to taking care of their families, they also performed back-breaking work in the fields.

The Abolitionist Movement

During the 1800s, the desire to end, or abolish, slavery began stirring the hearts of men and women. However, major abolitionist organizations barred women from membership since women couldn't participate in men's activities. Lucretia Mott heroically solved this problem in 1833 when she created the Philadelphia Female Anti-Slavery Society. For the first time in U.S. history, women worked together towards a common goal. Soon, other cities developed women's abolitionist organizations.

Go On

But male abolitionist organizations disliked the idea of women organizing. They tried to keep women out of the fight against slavery. Things came to a head in 1840 when Lucretia Mott and Elizabeth Cady Stanton were shut out of the World Anti-Slavery Convention. Many women decided then that until women enjoyed the same rights as men, they'd never be able to create any change at all.

The Seneca Falls Convention

Many female abolitionists organized a meeting in July 1848 in Seneca Falls, New York, to discuss the creation of legal rights for women. Both men and women attended the convention, including Frederick Douglass, a famous African American Abolitionist.

Elizabeth Cady Stanton read a "Declaration of Sentiments," based on the Declaration of Independence. For example, she stated that "all men and women are created equal" and then explained why women should "refuse allegiance" to an unfair government. Stanton's "Declaration" also listed goals, such as women's rights to vote, own property, keep wages, and receive an education. The suffragists were born!

A Long and Difficult Road

After the Seneca Falls, winning suffrage for women still took another 72 years to achieve. Elizabeth Cady Stanton and Lucretia Mott didn't live to see their dream realized. It wasn't until June 4, 1920 that the United States Senate passed the Anthony Amendment. It became the 19th Amendment to the Constitution and gave women the right to vote.

The years leading up to this point were long and difficult. Both sexes fought to keep the vote from women. The struggle broke apart families, caused violence, and ruined friendships. Critics thought the vote would take women's attention away from their husband and children. Others thought the right to vote would make women want other impossible things as well—such as to be president of the United States. While this goal has not yet come to pass, perhaps one day it will.

11 Which information would fit best under the heading "A Long and Difficult Road"?

  A how suffragists often protested in front of the White House

  B how the Underground Railroad helped to free slaves

  C where the World Anti-Slavery Convention took place

  D how many people attended the Seneca Falls Convention

12 How is this article organized?

  F It gives step-by-step instructions.

  G It gives descriptions of the suffragists.

  H It uses a question-and-answer format.

  J It tells events in the order they happened.

13 The section "Background History" is mostly about

  A the amendment that gave women the right to vote

  B why the Seneca Falls Convention was important

  C how women had few rights in the 1700s

  D how the abolitionist movement began

Go On 329

14 The author of this article would probably agree with which statement?

  F Only men should make decisions about how to amend the U.S. Constitution.

  G Women should never be president of the United States.

  H All U.S. citizens deserve the right to vote.

  J Girls and women in 1776 enjoyed more freedom than they do today.

15 The author says that the "the desire to end, or abolish, slavery began stirring the hearts of men and women" to show that

  A most people in the 1800s didn't have an opinion about slavery

  B men and women felt very differently about the topic of slavery

  C no one in the 1800s knew how to abolish the practice of slavery

  D the topic of slavery caused strong feelings in people

Read this story. Then answer questions 16 through 21.

The Way Things Were
by Tabitha Witherspoon

"**B**ring Your Pet to School Day" fell on the hottest day of the year—at least the hottest day of the year so far, since it was still only May.

"Remember to bring in Fido or Rover tomorrow," Mr. Feldman had reminded us the day before with a twinkle in his eye. Some said Mr. Feldman marched to his own beat, but I liked him, most of the time.

My feet stuck to the asphalt as I walked to school that morning, happy I'd left my goldfish Freddy at home. The water in his bowl would be boiling by now.

"Hey, Collins!"

I turned to see Charlie Peterson bearing down on me. The shimmering heat made Charlie look twice as big as usual. He was the biggest kid in my class. Groaning, I slowed down.

"Where's your iguana?" Charlie smirked.

Go On 331

"Goldfish," I replied. "Where's your dog?" I knew this wasn't nice since Charlie's dog had just died last year. But Charlie was the kind of person who made you not want to be nice on purpose.

This was because Charlie was always right, no matter what. For example, Charlie had known it wouldn't rain for our class trip to the Bronx Zoo—despite what the weatherman said—because he'd correctly identified the stratus as we lined up to get on the bus. One day, Charlie had saved our class from a geography pop quiz by sending Mr. Feldman powerful, anti-quiz thoughts the night before.

Now Charlie just grunted. "I wish I could bring Rex to school. He was the smartest, best dog that ever lived."

"Yeah," I said, not that I agreed. I avoided conflict with Charlie. Don't quote me, but part of the reason Charlie was right so much was because he looked and acted kind of scary when he wasn't right. His blue eyes bulged and his face turned the color of over-cooked beets. Even the girls avoided disagreeing with Charlie.

So for the whole school year, Charlie went on being right about everything. We all got used to it, and nobody even cared much. None of us talked about it or anything. It was just THE WAY THINGS WERE.

Soon, the schoolyard came into view. I noticed that only a few kids shared Mr. Feldman's enthusiasm for Bring Your Pet to School Day. Standing by the swing set, Amin was showing Mr. Feldman his pet boa constrictor, Carl. Alice sat nearby with her Dalmatian puppy. Blinking the sweat out of my eyes, I thought I saw Marion holding a hamster, but couldn't be sure.

"This is lame," Charlie said. "I wish Rex was here."

"Hey Toby!" I looked up to see Trevor leading a very large dog on a leash. Trevor had just moved to our school from Seattle. When Trevor stopped walking, the huge dog stopped, too, although he didn't look too happy about it. "This is Buddy," Trevor said.

I took a step back.

"I didn't know you had a dog. Did you bring him from Seattle?" asked Charlie.

"No," Trevor shook his head. His hair was so short he almost looked bald. And his skin was so pale you could see tiny blue veins running along underneath his skin like little streams. It made me nervous just looking at him, like I could break him if I coughed too hard. "A friend of my mom's couldn't keep him in her apartment." Trevor laughed, "He scared the neighbors."

"This old dog?" Charlie scoffed. "He looks like his dentures would fall out if he tried to bite someone."

Trevor tugged on the leash. "Actually, he's only a year old. He hasn't been around people much, and gets a little nervous in crowds, but my mom and I have been working with him." No one had ever told Trevor about Charlie always being right. I doubt anyone had ever even thought to tell him about it.

Trevor continued, "I brought him to school in order to train him, but promised Mr. Feldman I'd keep him on a short leash."

Charlie took a step closer. "I know all about dogs," he said. Buddy made a low, rumbling sound like a car engine turning over. "You should stay back," Trevor said quickly.

"I know all about dogs," Charlie repeated, but suddenly he didn't look so sure.

"I'm not kidding, Charlie. Stay back," Trevor said, while trying to keep Buddy relaxed.

"I'm just going to say hello to him. Then he'll know I'm his friend. He won't bite me," Charlie said, inching closer to Buddy.

As I watched Charlie get closer to the unhappy dog, I felt a flash of justice. Finally, Charlie would not be right this time around. But then I saw his face. I suddenly understood for the first time how much he missed his dog, Rex. That's what this was all about. I grabbed the back of Charlie's shirt before he could get any closer.

"Hey, wait a minute, Charlie," I said. "You need to be careful."

Go On

16 Which of the following statements is the **best** summary of this story's theme?

   F There is more to people than what we see on the surface.

   G Be true to yourself, no matter what.

   H Some people aren't meant to be friends.

   J You can't buy happiness.

17 Read this quote from Trevor.

> **"I brought him to school in order to train him, but promised
> Mr. Feldman I'd keep him on a short leash."**

Which meaning of "train" is used in this sentence?

   A a series or row of objects

   B to teach an animal to behave

   C the long part of a skirt or dress

   D a group of connected railroad cars

18 The style and wording of the story show that the author is

   F trying to make the reader sad

   G telling a story about an event

   H asking the reader to agree with her

   J encouraging the reader to learn more about dogs

19 The author compares Trevor's veins to

   A dogs

   B leashes

   C crowds

   D streams

20 Charlie would **best** be described as

    F   scary and hot-tempered

    G   friendly but foolish

    H   impatient but reasonable

    J   brave and funny

21 How do Toby's feelings about Charlie change at the end of the story? Use details from the story to support your answer.

_____

_____

_____

_____

_____

_____

STOP

POSTTEST

English
Language Arts
BOOK 2

TIPS FOR TAKING THE TEST

Here are some suggestions to help you do your best:

- Be sure to read carefully all the directions in the test book.

- Plan your time.

- Read each question carefully and think about the answer before choosing or writing your response.

Book 2

Part 1: Listening

Directions

In this part of the test, you are going to listen to an article called "A Traveling Dog." Then you will answer some questions about the article.

You will listen to the article twice. The first time you hear the article, listen carefully but do not take notes. As you listen to the article the second time, you may want to take notes. Use the space below and on the next page for your notes. You may use these notes to answer the questions that follow. Your notes on these pages will NOT count toward your final score.

For the multiple-choice questions, you will mark your answers on the answer sheet. For questions 26 and 27, you will write your answers directly in the book.

Notes

Go On 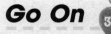 339

Notes

STOP

Book 2: Part 1

Do NOT turn this page until you are told to do so.

NOTICE: Photocopying any part of this book is forbidden by law.

341

Book 2: Part 1

22   Which sentence from the article states an opinion?

A   "He played a colorful role in the history of the U.S. Mail Rail System."

B   "Pony Express riders did get the mail to the far edges of the western frontier."

C   "He became the unofficial mascot of the U.S. Postal Service."

D   "He soon began hopping mail trains and traveling around New York."

23   Why did the author most likely write the article?

F   to encourage readers to use the U.S. Postal Service

G   to inform readers about an interesting part of U.S. Postal Service history

H   to describe how Pony Express Riders delivered the mail

J   to explain why dogs enjoy traveling by train

24   The web below shows states where Owney traveled.

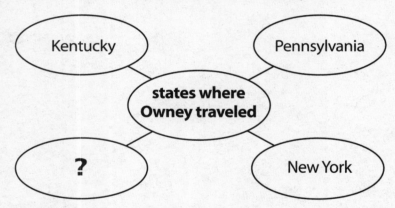

Which state best completes the web?

A   California

B   Washington

C   New Mexico

D   New Hampshire

25 Which of the following describes how Owney became the unofficial mascot of the U.S. Postal Service?

    F   He rode with the Pony Express.

    G   He helped deliver the mail to settlers out west.

    H   He rode the rail mail trains across the country for nine years.

    J   He belonged to the Postmaster, John Wanamaker.

26 Why do you think the U.S. Postal Service made Owney its unofficial mascot? Use details from the story to support your answer.

_____

_____

_____

_____

_____

STOP

Book 2

Part 2: Writing

Directions

On this part of the test, you will edit some paragraphs to correct errors. The entire class will work with your teacher on the Practice paragraph. Then you will correct the Editing Task on your own.

Sample

There are some mistakes in this paragraph. Let's correct them together.

When the weather report predicts the blizzard, nearly everyone hurried to stores to buy food batteries, and snow shovels. Cars crowded the roads leading in and out of syracuse. A few drivers cut off their neighbors in their rush to get home. Tempers flared. Several impatient drivers received Traffic Tickets. For speeding. But in the end, most people made it home before the storm.

Editing Task

27 Here is a paragraph a student wrote. There are some mistakes in the paragraph. Some sentences may have more than one mistake, and other sentences may contain no mistakes at all. There are <u>no</u> mistakes in spelling.

Read the paragraph and find the mistakes. Draw a line through each mistake in the paragraph. Then write the correction above it.

On Saturday, I went to see the new Movie everyone have been talking about. I expect it to be fantastic, but I ended up very disappointed. The plot was silly, I think even four-year-olds would have been bored. The worst part were the acting, though. It's like the actors were acting in their sleep. I walked out of the Theater wishing I could get a refund!

STOP

Glossary

argument   the position of the author and reasons for this view.

atlas   a book of maps.

ballad   an old form of song that tells a story, often about something sad or tragic.

bibliography   the list of resources used in researching a paper.

brainstorm   to think of different ideas for writing.

caption   a phrase or sentence that describes what is shown in a graphic.

CD-ROM   a compact disk read-only memory; contains information for use on a computer.

characterization   the development of characters in a story.

chronological order   a method of organizing text by placing events in the order they occur.

clause   a group of words with a subject and a predicate that expresses a thought.

climax   in fiction, the point at which the conflict is addressed by the main character(s); the most exciting part of the story.

comedy   a light-hearted drama written to entertain the audience.

comma   (,) the punctuation mark used to indicate a pause in a list of items, to set off a direct quotation, or before a conjunction when linking two independent clauses.

comparative   a word that suggests a comparison, such as *better*, *nicer*, or *smarter*.

compound sentence   two (or more) simple sentences put together; has two (or more) clauses, and two (or more) subjects, predicates, and ideas.

conclusion   an overall opinion that you form after reading a passage; a short paragraph that summarizes an essay and reminds the reader of the thesis statement.

conflict   the struggle or problem faced by the characters in a story.

context clues   the details in the sentence and paragraph that help you figure out what a word means.

coordinating conjunction   a word such as "and" or "but" that joins two words or clauses in a compound sentence.

couplet   a pair of lines with end rhymes.

dependent clause   a clause that cannot stand on its own as a sentence; also called a subordinate clause.

dialect   an individual's spoken style of language, including the words they use and their grammar and pronunciation.

dialogue   the written form for speech in fiction and drama.

diction   word choice; can be formal, middle, or informal.

dictionary   a book that lists the different definitions of a word and shows you the proper way to pronounce the word.

drama   writing meant to be performed by actors on a stage; the form includes dialogue and stage directions.

editorial   a form of nonfiction writing that expresses the writer's opinion about a subject.

encyclopedia   a book or series of books with alphabetical listings of topics with a short article on each.

essential information   information that is connected directly to the topic or to the argument or story of the passage.

fable   a brief story that teaches a lesson or moral; usually features animal characters.

fact   a statement whose validity, or truth, can be proved.

fairy tale   a made-up story featuring magical elements, such as fairies and enchanted creatures.

fiction   any type of story that describes imaginary people or events, or that tells a tale that is not factual.

figurative meaning   the imaginative, creative interpretation of a word, phrase, or sentence.

foreshadowing   the use of clues to hint at future events or the outcome of the story.

formal diction   an impersonal word choice that uses complex words.

freewriting   an exercise in prewriting in which you write about your topic for a set period of time without interruption.

glossary   an alphabetical collection of terms used in a book.

graphic organizer   a set of connected boxes (or circles) that help you visualize your ideas.

haiku   a traditional Japanese form of poetry consisting of 17 syllables.

heading   a group of words that divides text to tell the reader what the section they are reading is about.

imagery   the words in a literary work that appeal to one or more of the senses: sight, taste, touch, hearing, and smell.

independent clause   a clause that can stand on its own as a sentence; also called a main clause.

index   an alphabetical lists of subjects mentioned in the book, followed by the number on the page on which the subject is mentioned.

inference   an educated guess based on available information, such as details in the passage, prior knowledge, and common sense.

informal diction   the language used in everyday speech, including simple, common words, contractions, and figures of speech.

informational text   any text written with the purpose of educating the reader about something.

Internet   an electronic collection of sources that you access through a computer.

introduction   the paragraph explaining the essay topic and thesis, written to grab the reader's attention.

legend   a story that has been passed down for generations; usually an exaggerated version about someone real.

limerick   a humorous, rhyming poem of five lines.

literal meaning   the exact, specific meaning of a word.

lyric   a poem originally written to be sung.

main idea   what a passage is mostly about.

metaphor   a figure of speech in which one thing is described in terms of another, often (but not always) using a version of the verb "to be."

meter   the pattern of rhythm in a poem.

middle diction   word choice with correct usage; best represents the speech of a well-educated person.

myth   a traditional story featuring heroes or supernatural beings, often exploring the origins of things.

nonessential information   information that is not important to the topic, to the argument of the passage, or to the story being told.

nonfiction   any writing that describes actual people or events; the form includes sentences and paragraphs.

novel   a long work of fiction that includes plot, setting, and characters.

ode   a type of lyric poetry in praise of someone or something.

opinion   an individual's personal belief about a subject, which cannot be proven true or false.

paraphrase   using your own words to describe what happened in a text.

periodicals   the publications that are published at regular time intervals, such as daily, weekly, or quarterly.

personification   to give human qualities to something that is not human, like an animal or object.

plot   what happens in a story.

poetry   expressive writing that uses rhythm and rhyme to convey emotion; the form uses stanzas, or groups of lines.

predicate   part of a sentence that includes the verb and describes something the subject is or does.

prewriting   any preparation for writing, including brainstorming, freewriting, collecting information, and organizing ideas.

prior knowledge   what you already know as you begin to read or write.

quotations   the exact words a person or source uses, shown within quotation marks.

resolution   in fiction, how the conflict is resolved.

review   a nonfiction article with opinions about a book, play, movie, restaurant, concert, or event.

rhyme   when words end with the same sound.

rhythm   in poetry, the use of stressed and unstressed syllables to create a beat.

rising action   in fiction, the events that follow the conflict and lead up to the story's climax; often the bulk of the story.

sentence fragment   a sentence lacking a subject or predicate.

sentence variety   varying the length and style of sentences in writing.

sequence   a method of organizing a text by following the order of events.

setting   where and when a story takes place.

short story   a short work of fiction includes character(s), plot, setting, and theme.

simile   a comparison of two unlike things using either *as* or *like* as a connecting word.

simple sentence   a sentence made up of one independent clause.

sonnet   a rhymed lyric poem of 14 lines.

spelling   the standard or correct arrangement of letters to make a word.

stage directions   in drama, the instructions about setting and character action.

stanza   a group of lines in poetry.

subject   who or what a sentence is about.

subject-verb agreement   the use of a singular verb for a singular subject, and a plural verb for a plural subject.

summary   a brief description of a text in your own words.

superlative   a word that speaks in extremes, such as *all*, *everyone*, *best*, and *worst*.

supporting detail   information in a passage that supports the main idea.

supporting paragraph   a paragraph that backs up a thesis statement.

symbolism   a literary device that uses an object to represent a theme, idea, or emotion.

table of contents   a list of chapters, with page numbers, found at the beginning of a book.

theme   the central idea or meaning of a selection.

thesaurus   a book-length alphabetical list of words that gives their synonyms and antonyms.

thesis statement   a sentence that gives readers the main idea of an essay; usually the last sentence of the introduction.

topic sentence   the sentence in a paragraph that expresses its main idea.

tragedy   a drama that deals with serious subject matter and does not have a happy ending.

tragic flaw   the trait of the hero or heroine that brings him or her to their downfall in a tragedy.

Scoring Rubric for Short-Response Questions

Score	To get this score, the student—
2	wrote a response that is accurate and complete, and fulfills all the requirements of the task. Necessary support and/or examples are included, and the information given is clearly text-based. Any extensions beyond the text are relevant to the task.
1	wrote a response that includes some correct information, but may be too general or overly specific. Some of the support and/or examples may be incomplete or omitted.
0	wrote a response that is inaccurate, confused, and/or irrelevant, or the student failed to respond to the task.

Frequently Misspelled Words

Frequently Misspelled Words	
Proper Spelling	**Common Misspellings**
about	uhbowt, abot, abowt
action	ackshun, akshun, actshunadres,
address	addres, adress
again	uhgen, agin, agan, agen
always	allways, alwayze, alweys, alweeze
balloon	belloon, baloon, ballon, ballune
bought	bawt, buoght, boght
because	beecause, becuz, becase
before	beefor, befor, befour, beefour
been	bin, ben, bene
calendar	calendir, calender, celendar, celindir
children	chilldrun, childrin, childron, childrun
choose	chose, chews, chewz
color	culur, coler, colar, colir
could	cud, cood
come	kum, kome
doctor	ductor, docter, doctar, doctir, dacter
enough	enuf, enuff, enogh, enuogh
every	evre, evrre, everry, evry
favorite	favrit, faverite, favirite
friend	frend, freind
great	grate, gret, grat
listen	lissn, lissen, listin, lissin
loose	lose, lews, lows, loows
maybe	maybee, mebee, mabe, maby
peace, piece	peece, peas, peize, peeze
principle, principal	prinsipal, principul, prinzipel, prinseple
receive	recieve, receeve

Reading List

Title	Author
The Wizard of Oz	Baum, L. Frank
Tales of a 4th Grade Nothing	Blume, Judy
The Pinballs	Byars, Betsy
The Secret Garden	Burnett, Frances Hodgson
Stories Julian Tells	Cameron, Ann
Sadako and the Thousand Paper Cranes	Coerr, Eleanor
Ben and Me	Lawson, Robert
Jelly Belly	Lee, Dennis
Pippi Longstocking	Lindgren, Astrid
Sarah, Plain and Tall	MacLachlan, Patricia
Shiloh	Naylor, Phyllis Reynolds
Orphan Train Quartet	Nixon, Joan Lowery
The Great Gilly Hopkins	Paterson, Katherine
Soup	Peck, Robert Newton
Where the Red Fern Grows	Rawls, William
Shades of Gray	Reeder, Carolyn
Appalachia: Voices of the Sleeping Birds	Rylant, Cynthia
Wayside School	Sacher, Louis
Knights of the Kitchen Table	Scieszka, Jon
The Nate the Great Series	Sharmat, Marjorie
Mostly Michael	Smith, Robert Kimmel
Sign of the Beaver	Speare, Elizabeth George
Maniac Magic	Spinelli, Jerry
Abel's Island	Steig, William
The Widow's Broom	Van Allsburg, Chris
Charlotte's Web	White, E. B
Little House on the Prairie	Wilder, Laura Ingalls
The Velveteen Rabbit	Williams, Marjorie
Molly's Pilgrim	Cohen, Barbara
From Sea to Shining Sea	Cohn, Amy T.
Three Perfect Peaches	DeFelice, Cynthia
The People Could Fly	Hamilton, Virginia
The Legend of Sleepy Hollow	Irving, Washington

NEW YORK STATE Coach

America's Best for Student Success

JUMPSTART

English Language Arts

GRADE 5

109NY

New York State Coach Jumpstart, English Language Arts, Grade 5
109NY
1-59823-342-4

EVP, Publisher: Bill Scroggie
VP, Editorial Director: Marie Spano
VP, Creative Director: Rosanne Guararra
VP of Production: Dina Goren
Art Director: Farzana Razak

Executive Editor: Justin Trewartha
Development Editor: Norma Brenes
Author: Cypress Curriculum Services, LLC
Senior Designer: Otto Carbajal
Cover Illustration: Lloyd Birmingham/Images.com

Triumph Learning® 136 Madison Avenue, 7th Floor, New York, NY 10016
© 2007 Triumph Learning, LLC
A Haights Cross Communications, Inc. company

Printed in the United States of America.

10 9 8 7 6 5 4 3 2 1

Table of Contents

Introduction

Each year, New York State gives students something called the **New York State English Language Arts Test**. So how do you get ready for this test? With this book: the ***New York State Coach Jumpstart, English Language Arts, Grade 5***.

There are three practice tests in this book. The Coached Test includes questions with hints that will help you find the right answer.

Enjoy reading the passages, and do your best answering the questions.

Good luck on the test!

New York State Coach Jumpstart, English Language Arts, Grade 5

BOOK 1

PRETEST

TIPS FOR TAKING THE TEST

Here are some suggestions to help you do your best:

- Be sure to read carefully all the directions in the test book.
- Plan your time.
- Read each question carefully and think about the answer before writing your response.

Coach
America's Best for Student Success

Book 1

◄ Reading

Directions

In this part of the test, you are going to do some reading.
Then you will answer questions about what you have read.

Read this story. Then answer questions 1 through 7.

The Rabbit and the Tar Wolf

Cherokee Oral Tradition

Once there was such a long spell of dry weather that there was no more water in the creeks and springs. The animals held a meeting to see what to do about it. One of them suggested that they build a well. Everyone agreed except the rabbit, who didn't want to get his paws dirty. The rabbit said, "I don't need to dig for water. The dew of the grass is enough for me." The others did not like this, but they went to work together and dug their well.

They noticed that the rabbit looked as fresh as a spring daisy. It seemed as if he was getting sufficient liquid refreshment. The water in the well was getting low. The animals said, "That tricky rabbit steals our water at night." They decided to trick the rabbit.

They made a wolf out of pine tree sap and tar and set it up by the well to scare the thief. That night the rabbit came to the well to drink enough water to last him all the next day. He saw the strange tar wolf by the well and said, "Who's there?" but the tar wolf said nothing. The rabbit came closer, but the wolf never moved. So the rabbit came up and struck it with his paw. The pine gum held his paw and it stuck fast. Now he was angry and said, "Let me go or I'll kick you." Still the wolf remained silent. Then the rabbit struck again with his hind foot. He hit so hard that his foot was also caught in the gum and he could not move. He was trapped there until the other animals came for water the next morning. When they found out who the thief was, they agreed to put him in jail. However, as soon as they unstuck the rabbit, he quickly hopped away.

---

1 What is the **main** problem in the passage?

A The rabbit is stuck to the tar wolf.

B The animals do not have any water.

C The rabbit will not cooperate.

D Someone is stealing water from the well.

2 Read this sentence from the passage.

They noticed that the rabbit looked as fresh as a spring daisy.

This sentence is an example of

F personification

G metaphor

H simile

J contrast

Go On

3 What is the setting for the events in the passage?

A the zoo

B the desert

C the beach

D the forest

4 The rabbit can **best** be described as

F tired

G honest

H helpful

J selfish

5 Why did the animals build the tar wolf?

A to catch the thief

B to bite the thief

C to attract other animals to the well

D to help dig the well

6 Which of these statements **best** summarizes what the rabbit learns at the end of the story?

F Friends are important.

G Don't steal from others.

H Don't talk to strangers.

J A tar wolf is easy to make.

7 Read this sentence from the passage.

It seemed as if he was getting sufficient liquid refreshment.

What does the word "sufficient" mean?

A quick

B enough

C scarce

D usual

Directions

Read this article about a fair. Then answer questions 8 through 14.

The 1939 New York World's Fair

by Michelle Underwood

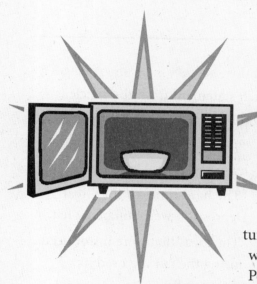

When you think of a fair, what do you imagine? Do you think of cotton candy and Ferris wheels, carnival games and animal shows? This is what usually comes to mind, but at the 1939 World's Fair, things were much different.

The World's Fair was an exposition of new ideas for the public. This was how people could learn about new inventions. Today, we can just turn on our televisions to see what's going on in the world. But in the 1930s there weren't any televisions. People had to depend on the newspaper, radio, and events like the World's Fair for information.

Many of the things that are in our houses today were only imagined at the time of the 1939 World's Fair in New York. At the World's Fair, people brought new inventions and new ideas to introduce to society. The world is a better place today because of these new technologies.

This time in history reminds most people of a period of unrest and hardship. The hard times of the Great Depression were still being felt. Europe was preparing to go to war. Many of the exhibitors at the fair concentrated on looking to the future. They promised people only good things on the horizon. The 1939 World's Fair changed a time of sadness and struggle into a time of excitement and wonder.

Go On

The ideas that were introduced during the fair are used in society today. For the first time, visitors to the World's Fair in New York saw that they could have televisions in their homes. Of course, those televisions were black-and-white. The first television speech by a U.S. president was at the 1939 World's Fair. People were introduced to microwave ovens that would cook food in less than a second! Computers and copy machines to make work easier and faster were exhibited. People would also see jet planes as a way of travel for the first time. These were just a few of the many new ideas for the future that captured people's imagination.

8 Why did the author **most likely** write this passage?

F   to explain the history of the computer

G   to show how much fun fairs can be

H   to talk about the 1939 World's Fair

J   to talk about New York in 1939

9 Read this sentence from the article.

The World's Fair was an exposition of new ideas for the public.

An "exposition" is most likely

A   a book

B   a game

C   a party

D   a display

10 Which statement from the article is an **opinion**?

F   "This was how people could learn about new inventions."

G   "The hard times of the Great Depression were still being felt."

H   "The ideas that were introduced during the fair are used in society today."

J   "The world is a better place today because of these new technologies."

11 According to the article, all of these inventions were seen at the 1939 World's Fair **except**

A   televisions

B   computers

C   lasers

D   jet planes

12 The passage shows that the author thinks that

    F   the World's Fair was exciting

    G   the World's Fair was boring

    H   the World's Fair cost too much

    J   the World's Fair confused visitors

13 Which idea from the article is **not** believable?

    A   fairs with no cotton candy

    B   no television in the 1930s

    C   exhibits that focused on the future

    D   microwave ovens that cooked food in less than a second

14 Complete the chart below by giving **two** inventions from the World's Fair in 1939 and **two** ways that those same inventions have changed today.

Inventions at the World's Fair in 1939	Those same inventions today
1.	1.
2.	2.

Go On

Duplicating any part of this book is prohibited by law.   Book 1   11

Directions
Read this passage. Then answer questions 15 through 21.

Mercury and the Woodsman

Adapted from Aesop's Fables

A woodsman was attempting to cut down a tree on the bank of a river. It seemed, though, that the tree had other ideas. The woodsman's axe glanced off the trunk, flew out of his hands, and fell into the water. The woodsman felt as if he had lost his best friend. As he sat glumly on the grass by the water's edge, the god Mercury appeared. "Why are you sad?" asked Mercury. The woodsman explained how he had lost his axe.

Feeling pity for the woodsman, Mercury dove into the river and grabbed a golden axe. "Is this the axe you lost?" Mercury asked the woodsman.

"No, that isn't my axe," the woodsman replied.

Mercury dove a second time and brought up a silver axe. "Is this one yours?" he asked.

"No, that is not mine, either," said the woodsman.

Once more Mercury dove into the river. This time he brought up the missing axe. The woodsman was overjoyed and thanked Mercury warmly. Mercury was so impressed that the woodsman was so honest that he gave him the gold and silver axes, too.

Book 1

When the woodsman told the story, one of his friends was filled with envy. The woodsman's friend decided to try his luck with Mercury. He began to cut down a tree at the edge of the river and pretended to drop his axe into the water. Mercury appeared as before and dove into the water, bringing up a golden axe. Without waiting to be asked, the woodsman's friend cried, "That's mine! That's mine!" He stretched out his hand eagerly for the prize, but Mercury refused.

"A lost axe is all you will get for your dishonesty," said Mercury. Then he took the golden axe and disappeared into the woods.

---

15 Which of these acts **most** like a person?

A the tree

B the axe

C the river

D the grass

16 This passage is **most** like a

F news story

G ghost story

H fairy tale

J science fiction tale

17 Why does the woodsman's friend throw his axe in the water?

A to clean it

B to hide it

C to get a golden axe

D because he is angry

Go On

18 According to the story, what happened when the second woodsman lied?

  F Mercury refused to give him the golden axe.

  G Mercury turned the woodsman into a golden axe.

  H Mercury gave him back his axe.

  J Mercury banned him from cutting trees again.

19 What does the story reveal about Mercury?

  A He did not think people could change their ways.

  B He believed good people should be rewarded.

  C He did not think people should cut down trees.

  D He was forgiving of those who wronged him.

20 This passage is **mostly** about

  F cutting down trees

  G honesty and greed

  H losing an axe

  J ancient gods

21 How do the first woodsman's feelings change from the beginning of the story to the end?

  A They change from happiness to grief.

  B They change from sadness to joy.

  C They change from anger to relief.

  D They change from disbelief to delight.

STOP

New York State Coach Jumpstart, English Language Arts, Grade 5

BOOK 2

PRETEST

Coach
America's Best for Student Success

Book 2

Part 1: Listening

Directions

In this part of the test, you are going to listen to an article called "Endangered Plants and Animals." Then you will answer some questions about the article.

You will listen to the article twice. The first time you hear the article, listen carefully but do not take notes. As you listen to the article the second time, you may want to take notes. Use the space below and on the next page for your notes. You may use these notes to answer the questions that follow. Your notes on these pages will NOT count toward your final score.

Notes

Do NOT turn this page until you are told to do so.

22 Which statement **best** shows that it is important to protect endangered plants and animals?

    F   Endangered plants and animals need to be protected.

    G   When plants and animals are under threat of dying out, they are called "endangered."

    H   In the United States, there are 398 animals and 599 plants on the list.

    J   There are many animal species that will never walk the Earth again.

23 The article gives a list of "extinct animals." The word "extinct" means

    A   in danger

    B   living

    C   protected

    D   died out

24 According to the article, the American alligator is

    F   extinct

    G   endangered

    H   dangerous

    J   not in danger

    Book 2: Part 1

25 What does the article suggest about protecting endangered animals and plants?

   A   People can help by staying informed.

   B   It is up to the government to protect them.

   C   Too much money is wasted protecting them.

   D   Protecting animals is more important than protecting plants.

26 Summarize the relationship between endangered plants and animals and ecosystems. Use details from the article to support your answer.

_____

_____

_____

_____

_____

STOP

Book 2

Part 2: Writing

Sample

There are some mistakes in this paragraph. Let's correct them together.

> My cat is extremely lazy. It's difficult to get her to do anything. It seems that all she wanted to do is curl up on the rug and sleep. I buy her a lot of toys to try to get her to be more active. The problem is that she never wants to play with it. I am always going to love my cat. Because she is so sweet. I just wish She would get off the rug more often!

STOP

27 Here is a paragraph a student wrote. There are some mistakes in the paragraph. Some sentences may have more than one mistake, and other sentences may contain no mistakes at all. There are <u>no</u> mistakes in spelling.

Read the paragraph and find the mistakes. Draw a line through each mistake in the paragraph. Then write the correction above it.

At my school, we have pep rallies right before football games. Pep rallies are a way of getting everyone excited about a game. Students come out to cheer for his team. When we have pep rallies. we get dismissed from school a little early. It's a really fun day. Everyone laughs and cheering. We can't wait for the game to begin. As our team finally ran out on the field, we make a lot of noise. It is like a giant wave of sound. There is no place any of us would rather be.

STOP

New York State Coach Jumpstart, English Language Arts, Grade 5

BOOK 1

COACHED TEST

TIPS FOR TAKING THE TEST

Here are some suggestions to help you do your best:

- Be sure to read carefully all the directions in the test book.
- Plan your time.
- Read each question carefully and think about the answer before writing your response.

Coach
America's Best for Student Success

Book 1

Reading

Directions

In this part of the test, you are going to do some reading.
Then you will answer questions about what you have read.

Read this story about a cat. Then answer questions 1 through 7.

Why the Cat Falls on Her Feet

Adapted from a Native American Folktale

"I'm too tired to walk farther until I get some rest," said Tisha wearily. The sun was high overhead when Tisha lay down at the foot of a tree. As she rested, she heard the songs of the birds, the buzz and hum of insects, and the wind rustling leaves. A feeling of peace came over Tisha. Soon, the music of the forest lulled her to sleep.

While Tisha slept, a poisonous snake slid noiselessly through the grass. It lifted its head and saw Tisha lying at the foot of the tree. "I could have eaten that squirrel yesterday," it hissed, "if this woman hadn't called out, 'Watch out, little squirrel!' Now it will be her turn to feel my fangs!"

The snake slithered closer. Suddenly, Tisha mumbled in her sleep, "Watch out, little squirrel!" The snake heard this and pulled back. Soon it noticed that Tisha's eyes shut again. The snake prepared to strike.

On a high branch above Tisha's head sat a little cat. She saw the snake when it first slithered up. She watched it glide through the grass and draw closer to Tisha.

Book 1

The little cat thought, "Tisha has been very good to me. I cannot let the snake bite her." In the next instant, the cat leapt down onto the snake. Surprised and angry, the great snake hissed and its eyes were like balls of fire as it lashed out wildly at the cat. The little cat leapt again and again upon the snake's head until it lay dead beside Tisha.

When Tisha awoke, the cat was lying near the dead snake. Tisha realized that the cat had saved her life. She stroked her head gently and said, "You brave creature! You saved my life. What can I do to show my gratitude and to honor you for your brave fight?"

At last she exclaimed, "I know what I shall do! You have sharp eyes and keen ears. You can run swiftly. Hereafter, you shall be known over all the earth as the friend of people. You shall always have a home in people's homes. You jumped from the high tree to kill the poisonous snake. Now as long as you live, you shall be able to leap wherever you want and always land upon your feet."

COACHED TEST

---

1 What is Tisha's **main** problem in the second paragraph?

A She is hungry and cannot find food.

B She is sleeping as a snake approaches.

C A cat is about to jump on her head.

D She is bitten by a snake.

HINT Look back at the second paragraph. Read the details carefully.

2 Read this sentence from the passage.

As she rested, she heard the songs of the birds, the buzz and hum of insects, and the wind rustling leaves.

Which word imitates the sound associated with the word?

F leaves

G rested

H songs

J buzz

HINT Onomatopoeia refers to a word that sounds like its name, such as the word "hiss."

Go On

3 What is the setting for the events in the passage?

A the beach

B the zoo

C the forest

D a pet store

HINT Cross out any answers that you know are incorrect. Then choose from the remaining answers.

4 Tisha is **best** described as

F mean

G a good friend

H afraid of snakes

J lazy

HINT Remember why the little cat decided to save Tisha.

5 What kind of animal did Tisha save?

A a cat

B a monkey

C a squirrel

D a snake

HINT Remember what the snake said as it approached Tisha.

6 Which of these statements **best** summarizes what the cat in the tree learns at the end of the passage?

F It's dangerous to help a friend.

G It's good to help a friend.

H Snakes have special powers.

J Be careful about who you trust.

HINT Read each answer choice and compare it to the passage. Choose the answer best supported by the events in the story.

7 Read this sentence from the passage.

> At last she exclaimed, "I know what I shall do! You have sharp eyes and keen ears."

What does the word "keen" mean?

A finely tuned

B very large

C intelligent

D eager

HINT Use context for clues to the word's meaning.

Say No to Uniforms!

I have been a student here at East Riverside Middle School for two years. I have not had any complaints about the school until recently. We are now required to wear uniforms. I believe that this is a violation of our right to free speech. We can no longer choose what we want to wear to school.

The school's dress code has always had rules on how students should and should not dress. The rules are very clear on proper attire. For example, we can't wear shorts, and sneakers are not allowed on Assembly Day. I respect the dress code, and it should be enough. We do not need uniforms, too.

Students understand that the reason for instituting the new uniform rule was not to punish us. And it is true that wearing uniforms helps some students behave and pay attention in class. Still, making everyone in the school wear uniforms just to help a few students is unfair. It's like giving an entire class detention because a couple of students misbehaved.

In addition, the uniforms are costly to buy. It can cost hundreds of dollars to buy uniforms for just one student. Sometimes they are also difficult to find. Most stores don't carry school uniforms. With so many kids going to so few stores to buy uniforms, the uniforms are bound to run out. Most importantly, uniforms are against our right to free speech. We should be able to express our own style. If we have to wear uniforms to school, we won't have as much fun. The rule about school uniforms should be changed.

Beverly Johnson

Go On

8 Why did the author **most likely** write this passage?

F to show why clothes are important to her

G to inform about the costs of buying uniforms

H to convince the school to change its uniform rule

J to explain why students are not getting a good education

HINT Think about the author's goal. What is it that she wants?

9 Read this sentence from the passage.

Students understand that the reason for instituting the new uniform rule was not to punish us.

What does the word "instituting" mean?

A starting

B stopping

C changing

D forgetting

HINT Replace the word in the sentence with each answer choice. Choose the one that makes the most sense in the sentence.

10 Which statement from the passage is an **opinion**?

F "I have been a student here at East Riverside Middle School for two years."

G "If we have to wear uniforms to school, we won't have as much fun."

H "We can no longer choose what we want to wear to school."

J "The school's dress code has always had rules on how students should and should not dress."

HINT An opinion is a statement that cannot be proven. Not everyone will agree.

11 According to the passage, school uniforms are unfair for all of the following reasons **except**

A they violate free speech

B they are uncomfortable

C they cost too much

D they are hard to find

HINT Three of the answer choices appear in the passage.

12 The passage shows that the author believes that

F school uniforms are a form of punishment

G wearing uniforms may benefit some students

H it is best if everyone dresses alike

J too much freedom can be harmful to students

HINT Re-read the third paragraph. What does the author say about uniforms?

13 Which of the following statements does **not** logically support the author's argument?

A "If we have to wear uniforms to school, we won't have as much fun."

B "The rules are very clear on proper attire."

C "I believe that this is a violation of our right to free speech."

D "We can no longer choose what we want to wear to school."

HINT This statement does not help the author make her point convincingly.

14 Complete this chart that analyzes each argument the author makes against school uniforms. On the left side, write the argument. On the right, write **one** example or support for the argument.

Argument	Support
1.	1.
2.	2.
3.	3.

HINT Each paragraph after the introduction offers a different argument. Read each paragraph to see how the argument is supported.

Go On

Directions

Read this poem. Then answer questions 15 through 21.

CHICAGO POET

by Carl Sandburg

I saluted a nobody.
I saw him in a looking-glass.
He smiled—so did I.
He crumpled the skin on his forehead, frowning—so did I.
Everything I did he did.
I said, "Hello, I know you."
And I was a liar to say so.

Ah, this looking-glass man!
Liar, fool, dreamer, play-actor,
Soldier, dusty drinker of dust—
Ah! he will go with me
Down the dark stairway
When nobody else is looking,
When everybody else is gone.

He locks his elbow in mine,
I lose all—but not him.

Book 1

15 Which of these lines from the poem **most** makes it clear that the man in the looking-glass is the speaker?

A "I saluted a nobody"

B "He locks his elbow in mine"

C "Everything I did he did"

D "Soldier, dusty drinker of dust"

HINT A looking-glass is a mirror.

16 How is this poem written?

F Each pair of lines rhymes.

G The lines do not rhyme.

H Each line is a complete sentence.

J A phrase is repeated over and over.

HINT Rhyming poems have lines that end with the same sound.

17 Why does the speaker in the poem feel he is a liar for saying "Hello, I know you"?

A He is talking to someone he just met.

B He is never honest with himself.

C He sees himself for the first time.

D He feels that he does not know himself.

HINT Re-read both stanzas of the poem. Think about how the speaker feels.

COACHED TEST

Go On

18 Read this line from the poem.

   I lose all—but not him.

   This line means that the speaker

   F   wants to forget his past

   G   wants to be alone

   H   is always with himself

   J   has lost nearly everything he owns

   HINT   Use what the speaker says in the second stanza to choose the right answer.

19 The speaker feels that

   A   people are the same everywhere

   B   his life is perfect the way it is

   C   he can always depend on himself

   D   he can always count on others in times of need

   HINT   The wrong answers are not supported by the poem.

20 This poem is **mostly** about

   F   becoming a better person

   G   learning about oneself

   H   having a strange dream

   J   acting in a play

   HINT   To find the main idea, think about what the speaker says and what he does.

21 Why does the speaker say that he locks elbows with the man in the looking-glass?

   A   to show that they are always together

   B   to show that they must go their separate ways

   C   to prove that he is the stronger one

   D   to keep him from getting away

   HINT   The speaker does not physically join elbows with the man in the looking-glass.

STOP

New York State Coach Jumpstart, English Language Arts, Grade 5

BOOK 2

COACHED TEST

Coach

America's Best for Student Success

Book 2

Part 1: Listening

Directions

In this part of the test, you are going to listen to an article called "Rudyard Kipling." Then you will answer some questions about the article.

You will listen to the article twice. The first time you hear the article, listen carefully but do not take notes. As you listen to the article the second time, you may want to take notes. Use the space below and on the next page for your notes. You may use these notes to answer the questions that follow. Your notes on these pages will NOT count toward your final score.

Notes

Do NOT turn this page until you are told to do so.

22 Which statement **best** shows that Rudyard Kipling was an important writer?

   F   Kipling was born in Bombay, India.

   G   Kipling wrote about life in India.

   H   Kipling received the Nobel Prize in 1907.

   J   Kipling worked as a journalist and editor.

HINT One of these shows that Kipling's writing was considered important.

23 The article says that "Kipling's poor eyesight and mediocre grades ended his hopes for a career in the military." The word "mediocre" means

   A   pretty good

   B   above-average

   C   not very good

   D   outstanding

HINT What kind of grades would have a negative effect on his hopes for a military career?

24 Which state did Kipling move to in the United States?

   F   New York

   G   Massachusetts

   H   Florida

   J   Vermont

HINT Review your notes to locate this information.

25 If Kipling had lived a great deal of his life in Italy instead of India, it is **most likely** that

    A   most of his novels would still be about India

    B   he would have written stories about life in Italy

    C   he would not have ended up in a foster home

    D   more people would be familiar with his writings

HINT   Base your answer on what you learned about Kipling and what makes the most sense.

26 Summarize the events in Kipling's life that **most likely** influenced his writings. Use details from the article to support your answer.

_____

_____

_____

_____

_____

_____

HINT   Think about the experiences most directly connected to Kipling's writings.

STOP

COACHED TEST

Book 2

Part 2: Writing

Sample

There are some mistakes in this paragraph. Let's correct them together.

> I love the view from my bedroom window. Every morning when I wake up. I look out at the trees decorated with leaves of many colors. One tree have been there for over 80 years. My grandmother used to climb it when she has been a little girl. I see a lot of birds, too. Their song wake me up sometimes, but I don't mind. It's better than waking up to an alarm clock.

STOP

27 Here is a paragraph a student wrote. There are some mistakes in the paragraph. Some sentences may have more than one mistake, and other sentences may contain no mistakes at all. There are <u>no</u> mistakes in spelling.

Read the paragraph and find the mistakes. Draw a line through each mistake in the paragraph. Then write the correction above it.

I've been collecting stamps since I was eight years old. I first got interested in stamps when I read an article called "Stamps of The World." The author described stamps from countries. Like England, Argentina, and Australia. She also included pictures of stamps. I found the article really interestingly. My father taken me to the library to get some books on stamp-collecting. I learned that people all over the world collect stamps. Before long, I was collecting stamps, too. I keep my stamps in a special book. They protect the stamps from wear and tear.

STOP

New York State Coach Jumpstart, English Language Arts, Grade 5

BOOK 1

POSTTEST

Tips for taking the test

Here are some suggestions to help you do your best:

- Be sure to read carefully all the directions in the test book.
- Plan your time.
- Read each question carefully and think about the answer before writing your response.

Coach
America's Best for Student Success

Book 1

Reading

Directions

In this part of the test, you are going to do some reading.
Then you will answer questions about what you have read.

Read this passage. Then answer questions 1 through 7.

Alice, Dinah, and Kitty

Adapted from Through the Looking Glass *by Lewis Carroll*

POSTTEST

"Oh, you wicked little thing!" cried Alice, picking up the kitten, and giving it a
little kiss to make it understand that it should be ashamed. "Really, Dinah ought
to have taught you better manners! You OUGHT to, Dinah, you know you ought
to!" she added, looking at the old cat and speaking in as angry a voice as she
could. Then she scrambled back into the armchair, taking the kitten and the yarn
with her. She began winding up the ball again. But she didn't get very far
because she was talking all the time, sometimes to the kitten and sometimes to
herself. Kitty sat very shyly on her knee. The kitten stared at the ball of yarn like
a child staring at a piece of chocolate.

"Do you know what tomorrow is, Kitty?" Alice began. "You'd have guessed if
you'd been up in the window with me—only Dinah was making
you tidy, so you couldn't. I was watching the boys picking up
sticks for the bonfire—and it needs plenty of sticks, Kitty! Only
it got so cold and it snowed so, they had to stop. Never mind,
Kitty, we'll go and see the bonfire tomorrow." Here, Alice wound
two or three turns of the yarn round the
kitten's neck, just to see how it would look.

Book 1

"Do you know, I was so angry, Kitty," Alice went on, "when I saw all the mischief you had been doing, I was very nearly opening the window, and putting you out into the snow! And you deserved it, you little mischievous darling! What have you got to say for yourself? Now don't interrupt me!" she went on, holding up one finger. "I'm going to tell you all your faults."

"Number one: you squeaked twice while Dinah was washing your face this morning. Now you can't deny it, Kitty, for I heard you! What's that you say?" (pretending that the kitten was speaking) "Her paw went into your eye? Well, that's *your* fault, for keeping your eyes open—if you'd shut them tight up, it wouldn't have happened. Now don't make any more excuses, but listen! Number two: you pulled Snowdrop away by the tail just as I had put down the saucer of milk before her! What, you were thirsty, were you? How do you know she wasn't thirsty, too?"

---

1 What is Alice's **main** problem in the first paragraph?

A Kitty has knocked a ball of yarn out of her hand.

B Dinah has knocked a ball of yarn out of her hand.

C She wanted a puppy, but got a cat instead.

D Kitty is making too much noise.

2 Read this sentence from the story.

The kitten stared at the ball of yarn like a child staring at a piece of chocolate.

The author means that the kitten

F wants to pounce on a piece of chocolate

G wants to eat something sweet

H wants to play with the yarn

J has never seen a ball of yarn before

Go On

3 What is the setting for the events in the story?

A a kitchen

B a backyard

C a house

D an animal hospital

4 Which word **best** describes Alice?

F amused

G forgetful

H talkative

J thankful

5 Why are the boys gathering sticks?

A to build a fence

B to make a bonfire

C to build a fort

D to make baskets

6 Which of these statements **best** summarizes what happens in the last paragraph?

F Dinah washes Kitty.

G Alice lets Kitty play with her yarn.

H Kitty pulls Snowdrop by the tail.

J Alice scolds Kitty.

7 Read this sentence from the story.

And you deserved it, you little mischievous darling!

What does the word "mischievous" mean?

A being sweet

B causing trouble

C making others laugh

D being harmless

Book 1

Directions

Read this article about the history of pizza. Then answer questions 8 through 14.

A Brief History of Pizza

by Andrew Romano

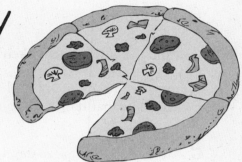

Pizza is the world's best meal. Pizza is a baked pie consisting of a shallow bread-like crust covered with tomato sauce, cheese, and often other toppings such as sausage, onions, mushrooms, and peppers. Pizza comes from Italy. The word *pizza* is believed to be from an Old Italian word meaning "a point."

Many different kinds of people lived in Italy thousands of years ago. Pizza might have been invented by any one of these groups. In one form or another, pizza has been a part of the Italian diet for a very long time. All Italians love pizza. The secret of pizza is mixing flour with water and heating it on a hot stone. The earliest form of pizza was crude bread that was baked beneath the coals of the fire. After cooking, it was seasoned with a variety of different toppings and used instead of plates and utensils to sop up broth or gravies. Working people and their families ate this bread because it was cheap and easy. It is believed that the idea of using bread as a plate came from the Greeks. They ate flat, round bread baked with different toppings.

In 1522, tomatoes were brought to Europe from Peru. By the late 1800s, tomato pizza was sold in the streets of Italy. It would be cut from a big tray in a baker's oven. As pizza became more popular, areas were set up where the dough was shaped as customers ordered. The early pizzerias were outdoor restaurants where people could sit together.

POSTTEST

Go On

Pizza came to America when many Italians moved here in the late 1800s. Chicago-style pizza was sold by a person who walked up and down the street with a metal bucket of pizzas on his head. This was the traditional way pizza was sold in Naples. The name of the pizzeria could be read on the bucket. Nowadays, people just walk into a pizzeria to get a slice.

---

8 Why did the author **most likely** write this article?

F   to show that Italy has a long history

G   to explain how pizza developed over time

H   to describe different Italian dishes

J   to get people to eat more pizza

9 Read this sentence from the article.

The earliest form of pizza was crude bread that was baked beneath the coals of the fire.

What does the word "crude" mean?

A   simple

B   fried

C   sliced

D   frozen

10 Which statement from the article is an **opinion**?

F   "In 1522, tomatoes were brought to Europe from Peru."

G   "Pizza comes from Italy."

H   "The name of the pizzeria could be read on the bucket."

J   "Pizza is the world's best meal."

11 According to the article, all of the following were part of making pizza what it is today **except**

A   tomatoes from Peru

B   pepperoni from Mexico

C   bread from Greece

D   hot stones

12 The passage shows that the author **most likely**

    F   is a history teacher

    G   has spent a great deal of time in Italy

    H   is proud that pizza has a long tradition

    J   enjoys traditional dishes from many countries

13 The author is **least** believable when he writes

    A   "In one form or another, pizza has been a part of the Italian diet for a very long time."

    B   "As pizza became more popular, areas were set up where the dough was shaped as customers ordered."

    C   "In 1522, tomatoes were brought to Europe from Peru."

    D   "All Italians love pizza."

14 Complete the chart below by filling in the causes and effects.

Cause	Effect
Greek people needed plates for food.	
	Crude bread was baked beneath the coals of the fire.
Tomatoes were brought from Peru.	

Go On

Directions

Read this story about a sprite. Then answer questions 15 through 21.

The Wicked Sprite

Adapted from The Snow Queen *by Hans Christian Andersen*

Once upon a time there was a wicked sprite. He was the most mischievous of all sprites. One day he was in a very good mood because he had made a mirror that made anything that was good or beautiful look ugly. And anything that was good-for-nothing and was truly ugly looked even uglier in the mirror. In this mirror, the most beautiful views of the outdoors looked like boiled spinach, and the best people were turned into frights. Their faces were so distorted that they could not be recognized. And if anyone had a freckle, you can be sure it would look much bigger and spread over the person's face.

"That's glorious fun!" said the sprite. All the little sprites that went to his school—he taught at a sprite school—were thrilled with the mirror. They could not wait to put it to use. They went everywhere with the mirror. At last there was not a place or a person who had not been distorted by the mirror. So then they thought they would fly up to the sky, and have a joke up there.

The higher they flew with the mirror, the more terribly it reflected. They could hardly hold onto it. Higher and higher still they flew, nearer and nearer to the stars, when suddenly the mirror shook so terribly that it flew out of their hands and fell to the earth. It was dashed in a hundred million and more pieces. Then the mirror worked much more evil than before. Some of those pieces were as small as a grain of sand, and they blew around in the wide world. When they got into people's eyes, there they stayed. Then those people saw everything distorted or evil. Even the very smallest bit had the same power of the whole mirror. The sprites danced when they saw this. Some people even got a splinter of the mirror in their heart, and then it was terrible. Their heart became a lump of ice. Some of the broken pieces were so large that they were used for windowpanes, through which a person could not see his friends. Other pieces were put in eyeglasses. It was sad when people put on their glasses hoping to see well. Then the wicked sprite laughed till he almost choked, for all this tickled his fancy.

15 Which of these sentences from the passage uses a metaphor?

A "Their heart became a lump of ice."

B "They could hardly hold onto it."

C "He was the most mischievous of all sprites."

D "Their faces were so distorted that they could not be recognized."

16 This passage is **most** like a

F short story

G poem

H news story

J fairy tale

Go On

17 What happened when people had a piece of the mirror in their eye?

 A They could see for miles.

 B They could not see anything.

 C They could see only evil.

 D They could see only good.

18 According to the passage, who did the wicked sprite tell about the mirror?

 F students at sprite school

 G people in town

 H people wearing eyeglasses

 J the leader of the sprites

19 The sprite is **most likely**

 A a very strong man

 B a flying horse

 C a magical creature

 D a wicked child

POSTTEST

Book 1

20 This passage is **mostly** about

    F   a sprite school

    G   a lucky mirror

    H   a nasty trick

    J   a funny sprite

21 This passage shows that

    A   things are not always what they appear to be

    B   people spend too much time in front of the mirror

    C   sprites do not want to hurt anyone

    D   sprites should stay in school

STOP

New York State Coach Jumpstart, English Language Arts, Grade 5

BOOK 2

POSTTEST

Coach™
America's Best for Student Success

Book 2

Part 1: Listening

Directions

In this part of the test, you are going to listen to an article called "Animals Helping People." Then you will answer some questions about the article.

You will listen to the article twice. The first time you hear the article, listen carefully but do not take notes. As you listen to the article the second time, you may want to take notes. Use the space below and on the next page for your notes. You may use these notes to answer the questions that follow. Your notes on these pages will NOT count toward your final score.

Here is a word you will need to know as you listen to the article.
therapy: treatment to cure or help people feel better

Notes

Do NOT turn this page until you are told to do so.

22 Which statement **best** shows that therapy animals can help people with disabilities?

    F   Therapy Animals is a group in Salt Lake City, Utah.

    G   Animals can help people in a way that other people cannot.

    H   Guide dogs look out for danger and warn people of obstacles.

    J   For most people, animals are mainly pets.

23 The article says that therapy dogs "provide a vital service to many." The word "vital" means

    A   unnecessary

    B   important

    C   expensive

    D   fast

24 Volunteers have children read to therapy dogs

    F   to make the children more relaxed

    G   to help train the dogs

    H   to prepare children for tests

    J   to see how smart the dogs are

POSTTEST

    Book 2: Part 1

25 Trainers of therapy dogs **most likely** choose dogs that

    A   are male

    B   bark a lot

    C   need help

    D   are gentle

26 Summarize the benefits of therapy dogs. Use details from the article to support your answer.

_____

_____

_____

_____

_____

_____

STOP

Book 2

Part 2: Writing

Sample

There are some mistakes in this paragraph. Let's correct them together.

> My brother is three years old, and he loves to watch TV. His favorite show is about a singing chihuahua. It's the silliest show I have ever saw in my entire life. I try to not be around when it's on, but sometimes I have no choice. I wish TV producers would make shows that is less silly. And annoying. Even toddlers deserve better choices!

STOP

27 Here is a paragraph a student wrote. There are some mistakes in the paragraph. Some sentences may have more than one mistake, and other sentences may contain no mistakes at all. There are <u>no</u> mistakes in spelling.

Read the paragraph and find the mistakes. Draw a line through each mistake in the paragraph. Then write the correction above it.

I love going to the Beach. I'm lucky to live near the coast. During the summer. I try to go every weekend. My friends and I pack the blankets, sandwiches, tanning lotion, and beach ball, and we head out for a day of fun. We have so much fun once we get there! We play ball, listen to music, dive in the ocean, and soaking up the sun. Sometimes I close my eyes, and the sound of the waves put me to sleep. When the day ended, we gather our belongings and go home.

STOP

POSTTEST

Notes

Notes

Notes